"IN THE MORNING WE WALK OUT-
SIDE and pray aloud together. Everybody
thinks that we are just talking, but then, we
are just talking—talking with the Saviour,
and there is such a joy!"

PRISON LETTERS is a collection of letters that
have miraculously survived to this day. Here are
the actual writings of Corrie and her sister Betsie
from the concentration camp . . . the emotion-
filled letters they received from relatives and
friends on the outside . . . all containing precious
lessons of faith and love learned in God's training
school.

It was only recently that Corrie herself reread
these moving letters, an experience that resur-
rected many painful memories for her. But with
the sadness came the conviction that God
wanted her to share these writings so that others
could experience the same faith that guided her
through a time of trial and triumph.

Bantam Books by Corrie ten Boom

THE HIDING PLACE
PRISON LETTERS

Corrie ten Boom's
PRISON LETTERS

*This low-priced Bantam Book
has been completely reset in a type face
designed for easy reading, and was printed
from new plates. It contains the complete
text of the original hard-cover edition.*
NOT ONE WORD HAS BEEN OMITTED.

▪

PRISON LETTERS

*A Bantam Book / published by arrangement with
Fleming H. Revell Company*

PRINTING HISTORY

Fleming H. Revell edition published May 1975
2nd printing .. September 1975   4th printing .... October 1976
3rd printing .... November 1975   5th printing .... April 1977

Bantam edition / September 1978

Scripture quotations not otherwise identified are from the
King James Version of the Bible.

Scripture quotation identified PHILLIPS is from *The New
Testament in Modern English*, translated by J. B. Phillips.
© J. B. Phillips 1958, 1960, 1972. Used by permission of
Macmillan Publishing Co., Inc.

Edited selections from *A Prisoner and Yet* . . . by Corrie
ten Boom are Copyright 1954 by Christian Literature Crusade,
London. Christian Literature Crusade, Fort Washington, 1975.
Used by permission.

ISBN 0-553-12020-4

Published simultaneously in the United States and Canada

---

*Bantam Books are published by Bantam Books, Inc. Its trade-
mark, consisting of the words "Bantam Books" and the por-
trayal of a bantam, is registered in the United States Patent
Office and in other countries. Marca Registrada. Bantam
Books, Inc., 666 Fifth Avenue, New York, New York 10019.*

PRINTED IN THE UNITED STATES OF AMERICA

To my family on earth
and in Heaven
whose testimony lives on through these letters
and through my life

Contents

These letters, sketches, and diary entries have been shared generously by Corrie ten Boom over the years. This material has been translated by different people at different times and in different places, and comparisons may sometimes suggest discrepancies in the presentations. All are agreed that the courage, the stamina, and the faith are undiminished—no matter the cell number, the date, or the interpretation.

Introduction

During the last world war as the German armies rolled over most of Europe, crushing countries in their path, Adolf Hitler set into operation a plan to exterminate all Jews. Many of the people of Holland responded by doing their utmost to help Dutch Jews to escape this peril. My own family and my friends and I did all that we could do to save Jewish lives until we were betrayed and arrested.

At that time, my father was eighty-four years of age and friends had often warned him that if he persisted in hiding Jews in his home under the very eye of the occupying armies, he could surely face imprisonment.

"I am too old for prison life," my father replied, "but if that should happen, then it would be, for me, an honor to give my life for God's ancient people, the Jews."

I recall with great clarity the day that we went down the winding staircase with our whole family and our friends. For some of them, it was the last time they would ever feel the worn staircase railing of the

1

beloved Beje—name for our home, located in the Barteljorisstraat—in their hands.

Father leaned heavily on my arm and, passing the large Frisian clock in the hall, he suggested that I pull up the weights to wind it. He could not realize that the next day when the clock unwound, there would be no one, only silence, in that so recently crowded, lively and joyful house, and that never again, as a family, would we enter Father's beloved house with its many clocks.

Thirty-five of our family and friends were led through the Smedestraat towards the police station that day. We then entered a large gymnastics room and sat down together as a family on one of the gymnasium mats which were spread out on the floor.

That night, God used Father to prepare each of us in a special way for the unknown times that lay ahead. Father asked my brother Willem to read Psalm 91 and then Father prayed.

"He that dwelleth in the secret place of the most High shall abide under the shadow of the Almighty.

"I will say of the Lord, He is my refuge and my fortress: my God; in him will I trust.

"Surely he shall deliver thee from the snare of the fowler, and from the noisome pestilence.

"He shall cover thee with his feathers, and under his wings shalt thou trust: his truth shall be thy shield and buckler."

That night in the police station was long and full of tension, but we were able to discuss the most important matters facing us. As we were loaded into the police van the next morning, on our way to the Scheveningen prison, people of our town of Haarlem were standing quietly in the street with tears in their eyes. It was the last time they would see Father, the "grand old man of Haarlem."

After an hour's ride, the van door opened and the gates of the prison closed behind us. We were ordered to stand with our faces pressed against the red brick wall. When our names were called, I passed by Father who was sitting on a chair. He looked up and we heard him softly saying, "The Lord be with you, my daughters."

From that moment forward, everything in our lives was changed. We did not know what was ahead of us, but I was certain of one thing—that Jesus would never leave us nor forsake us and that, for a child of God, no pit could be so deep that Jesus was not deeper still.

During my months of solitary confinement, I often felt lonely and afraid. In such moments I recalled that last night with my elderly father, sharing Psalm 91 and praying. I could remember some of those verses, especially that, "He shall cover thee with his feathers, and under his wings shalt thou trust: his truth shall be thy shield and buckler." I would close my eyes and visualize that kind of protection. "He shall cover thee with his feathers," and with that thought in mind, I would fall asleep.

The letters in the first half of this book were written from the Scheveningen prison where my sister Betsie was confined in a cell with other prisoners, while I was kept in solitary confinement. There are also letters that were sent to us by my sister Nollie and her husband, Flip, and their children; some written by my brother, Willem, and his wife, Tine, and their family; and others written by various relatives and friends. We were detained in Scheveningen from February 29, 1944 to June 5, 1944.

Prisoners were permitted to receive very few letters in both the Scheveningen prison and later in the Vught prison. Thus, sometimes many people might share in the writing of one letter, just as Betsie and I would write *one* letter to many people. The brief sketches in smaller type are added feelings of my own on life in the prisons. I was able to include them in letters smuggled out.

When, on June 6, Betsie and I were suddenly transported together to Vught, a German concentration camp in Holland, we were much happier in the sense that we were once again together after a long and difficult separation. I was in my early fifties then and Betsie was seven years older. Betsie was chronically ill from pernicious anemia and the prison diet adversely affected this disease, so that she was occasionally treated by a prison doctor. However, one only requested to see a doctor when very ill, for even the sickest patients were discouraged by such cruelties as having to stand at attention throughout their wait for medical help. Betsie and I had been very close over many years and had learned to depend on each other for many little things. It was a great comfort and blessing to be together at Vught and to no longer be confined to cells. Still, barracks life, with its long work hours under the pressures of both mental and physical cruelties, was not easy and our lives were in constant danger, for we were in the grip of an enemy who could, at the slightest whim, do whatever he wished with us. It was typical of the sadistic mind to provide, for show, the niceties of massage and other sophisticated medical care while, for the prisoner, punishment and relentless hunger and neglect were the routine practice.

Several letters were written from Vught. We were, technically, permitted to write one letter every two weeks. This letter was, of course, censored by prison authorities and, if individuals or groups were receiving special punishment, we could often neither send nor receive mail. Recognizing this censorship and also the great concern of our family for our well-being, we did not feel free to express in letters the harder side of prison life. However, in both the letters from Scheveningen and from Vught, we worked out a simple code for terms we felt would be censored or do us harm. I have explained some of this in brackets in the letters.

Most of the letters in this book were smuggled out of
Vught by a German soldier who hid them in clean
laundry that we prisoners washed for the Germans.
This young man also took the enclosed sketches for
me. Some of these I had written on toilet paper in
my cell at Scheveningen and hidden under my clothing all that time while in camp at Vught. I had the
opportunity, through this sympathetic soldier, to send
them to my sister. It was a dangerous procedure. If
one letter were intercepted, the penalty would be at
least prolonged imprisonment. But we took the risk
to send the letters and sketches out. Nollie saved every
note, including bits and pieces of a kind of diary
Betsie kept, and gave them to me after the war.

It was only a year ago that, after many years, I
read through all these letters and notes and saw what
a precious remembrance they are.

In September, 1944, the allied forces liberated part
of Holland. When they attacked the Germans in
Holland, countless numbers of Dutch prisoners were
hastily sent to Germany. Thousands were killed and
no one knows how many were transported in boxcars
to concentration camps deep in Germany. Many women were shipped to Ravensbruck, north of Berlin.
Prisoners there were forbidden contact with the outside world, and thus we have no letters from that
time.

I feel fortunate though, that the letters presented
here have been preserved. Many letters sent to Betsie
and me, and letters we wrote while in prison, of course

never did reach their destination. Other letters were so thoroughly censored that little was left of them.

But God, I know, helped to keep the ones in this book safe, surely for the purpose of my one day presenting them to others as a reminder of the great love He gave us and the comfort of His presence wherever we were.

1

Scheveningen

"How greatly a prison deprives people . . . ."

From time to time I wrote short sketches on scraps of paper. These were smuggled out and escaped censorship. The sketches are set in smaller print to separate them from the letters.

The Prison.

A cell consists of 4 stone walls and a closed door. There are 3 little holes through which we secretly talk and exchange little bits of prison news. It does not really bring us news, but it gives us the feeling that we are not sitting there completely separated. (In my previous cell I was with 3 other prisoners.) Then the guard entered with a prisoner, a real gentleman—cultured, silent. A container of cement was also brought in and there was a search for holes. They were found and closed with a dab of the concrete. On the way out, our little pencil was snatched away. The door closed again and we were locked in even more than before. How greatly a prison deprives people of the most elementary conditions of life! If God still grants me chances, I hope to work in the area of rehabilitation. I will now also dare to visit a prison cell, which I did not do before.

Here is the first of my letters to be received. The top of all our letters bore this warning:

Every three weeks both sides may send a letter. Cards are prohibited and will not get through. Letters without stamps are not accepted. (Write name and address of sender clearly.) Only toothpaste, toothbrush, and soap can be sent BY LETTER. Visits are not allowed. Clean laundry will be issued by the prison.

C. ten Boom, cell 384

April 11, 1944

Dear Nollie and all friends,

Thanks so much for Atie's parcel. It was perfect. All those colors! I am using the threads of the bath towel to embroider everything. I am fine. Have severe pleurisy but have improved much, except I am still coughing. I have miraculously adjusted to this lonely life, but I am in communion with God. I speak often with the Saviour. I am obtaining a deeper insight into time and eternity and am being prepared for both life and death. To depart and be with Christ is far better. But life with Him here on earth is also attractive. However I am longing to be more active.

The most difficult thing for me has been my worries about Betsie and especially Father. But then the Lord said, "Sheltered in my immeasurable love." Since then, I have no longer worried about them. I do worry about our customers' watches left in the empty house [Jews hidden in our secret room], but the Saviour is all the time averting all worry and fear and homesickness so that the doctor said to me, "You are always cheerful." I sing inside nearly all day long and we do have so much to be thankful for—an airy cell through which the sea wind blows, no more poverty since Atie's parcel arrived with its good food, three Red Cross sandwiches, half a pan of porridge extra, and then that continuous communion with the Saviour. I am grateful that I am alone, me who loves company and people so much! I see my sins more clearly, my own SELF in capitals, and much more superficiality in me. Once I asked to be freed but the Lord said, "My grace is sufficient for you." I am continuously looking at Him and trying not to be impatient. I won't be here one minute longer than God deems necessary. Pray for me that I can wait for His timing.

At Easter we received a royal parcel from the Red Cross with, among other things, smoked eel. If another parcel should still be necessary [if I am still in prison], please repeat all the food items, especially the Sanovite and Davitamon. The brown cake was a bit too hard. Send especially a dress with short sleeves, pajamas, colored bath towel, white thread, needle, thimble, vest and girdle and if possible, apples and soap from my black traveling case. [I had to leave my preplanned and prepacked emergency suitcase at home as it was sitting directly in front of the entrance to the secret room and I dared not draw attention to it. That was one of the greatest sacrifices I have ever had to make!]

Are Elske and Lenie still doing homework together?

Are Toetie and Mary still alive? Who is now taking
care of these animals? Are you allowed to visit Father
in the hospital? [My code for prison.] How are Hennie and Ineke? Write soon.

I am writing with a pen with only one point. I had
to go to a short hearing on March 8 and 28. Don't
know anything about the result yet. They were very
kind and asked little. Please write all you know about
Father and Bep. Life's dimensions here are very
strange. Time is something to be waded through. I
am surprised that I can adjust so well. To some things
I shall never get accustomed, but on the whole I am
really happy. Please never worry about me. Sometimes it may be dark, but the Saviour provides His
light and how wonderful that is. Bye now, dear, dear
people. Give my regards to all friends. Hope to see
you soon again, in God's time.

                                        YOUR CORRIE

Receiving a Parcel.

The Red Cross parcel is outside, near my door. It is a
contact by friendly people who are thinking of us and
maybe later will free us. Everybody has more courage on
the Wednesdays every two weeks when the Red Cross
parcels arrive.

The door opens. I get up and am standing on wobbly
legs. "Take it yourself! You are up anyway. I am not going
to hand it to you."

How depressing unkindness is!

I unpack it. The items are nice and tasty. They are
chosen by understanding people who knew what would

be good for us. Will this be the last parcel? In another two weeks we will be . . . ?

Look out, thoughts! Better concentrate and contemplate on the Saviour. With Him there is certainty. With the other only uncertainty and delayed hope which hurts the heart.

. . . biscuits, a croquette, licorice. But why is there no happiness in my heart? Alone.

To eat this or that candy alone. How depressing it is. I am planning to offer the *Wachtmeisterin* something but decide against it.

I think that later (will there be a later?) I won't ever like to eat candies alone by myself. Somebody will have to share and then I will think of cell 384.

Betsie was writing to our niece that very same day . . . .

E. ten Boom, cell 314

April 11, 1944

Dear Cocky   (Continue to pray fervently for me.)

So our dear father has now been promoted to Glory. And how? The Lord Himself crowned his head with the martyr's crown. Many years ago I had a premonition of this, but I steadfastly put it out of my mind. I often thought that a person in whom Christ was shown to such full advantage, who lived so close to the Saviour, to whom the eternal things were so real, and who had the gift of prayer in such a wonderful way—such a person has all the conditions for becoming a martyr. And then I thought, "He is not going to die in his bed." All this only came back to mind after he had died. The Lord gave him a happy life, such as not one in 10,000 has. Just before his death the Lord took him away from his dear ones in order to be able to give him the crown of honor. God did not let His Sovereignty slip from His fingers. No, this all had to be this way, even my being here in prison. I can also see this from the few preparations which I unconsciously made—among other things the many clothes I had on that I never ordinarily wore, also the fact that I was not allowed to take my glasses along. For now I have so much more opportunity to pray for all the family and friends than I ever had before in my busy life. Yes, I received the glasses on Easter Sunday morning. I cannot read with these. However, I can sew with them and enjoy doing that immensely. There is a kind teacher with me who daily reads to me from my old friend, *David Copperfield,* and I enjoy it. She also combed my hair with a fine comb, with results, and she is now writing for me.

Cocky, tell everybody who is praying for me that they should especially thank God because miracles are happening here every day. The rush of great waters came at me, but I did not despair for one moment. The Lord is close to me as never before in my life. Even in those first terrible days I felt His nearness and knew that this was not punishment for He suffered completely for me at Golgotha. But that this horror had come to us from His loving hand to purify me. From the first moment on, I have been able to adjust to my cell and to prison life. I sleep well, and do not suffer from cold, except that my feet were cold at first. Due to nervousness, my stomach could not tolerate the prison food. I hardly ate anything and was suffering from hunger. After 4 weeks of that I asked to see the doctor and now I am getting delicious porridge and things are going better.

We struggle daily in the cell to keep the cell, body, and clothes clean. The days fly. As time passes everything improves. Also the parcel helped, Cocky. Give my regards to your mother. [Nollie is still in prison.] I am longing so much for you and for news from Willem, Peter, Corrie [all in prison]. Now I can peacefully look forward to the future and the interrogation (on April 19th). May the Lord soon give deliverance.

BETSIE

Betsie hears from home . . . .

April 21, 1944

Dear Bep,

Your letter gave me so much consolation. I was worrying so much about your sorrow. We are now writing it to Corrie. She still does not know anything. She also wrote in good spirits. She is feeling much better but still has been coughing. She is talking much with the Saviour and is getting a deeper insight into time and eternity.

Where are your good glasses? Tine received notice that Willem will be home soon. We got a wonderful

letter from Peter (from prison). The shop and the
repair shop are open. Much has been stolen from the
house and they broke into the shop. Henri is managing
the shop. The house is still sealed up. Flip is apparently coming May 1st and will go to school. We pray
much for you both. Please also pray for me, for it is
much more difficult for me now than when I was
in Scheveningen. I was in a cell there with Aukje.
We had a good time. Aukje is still there. Mary was
taken care of in her home. Yesterday I was in
Scheveningen, where I had to go to get Father's belongings. I am so grateful that you are doing well.
Come immediately to us when you are free. How
good we will be to you! God bless you darling!

YOUR NOLLIE

Best regards and lots of strength.

FLIP

Many regards.

PIET

Dear Aunt Bep,

What a wonderful letter. And everybody in such
good spirits. Aukje just got out. She is fine. Best
wishes from Frits and Dora. They are fine. We hope
and pray for a speedy homecoming. How wonderful
that will be. It was such a consolation for us the way
you accepted Grandfather's passing away. Mother only

heard it after she came home. It was such a great
sorrow for her. Now she is doing a bit better. Well,
dear Aunt, strength and God's blessing. Love from,

ATY

Dear Aunt Bep,

How happy we are with your letter. Now we hope
that you may return soon. An elderly lady is taking
care of Toetie. Bye for now, dear Aunt. All the best.
Kind regards and a kiss.

ELSKE

Best regards and strength.

UNCLE JOOP

Dear Aunt Bep,

What a surprise! Three letters at the same time—
from Peter, Aunt Kees, and from you. How wonderful
that you are feeling so well! Everything is going well
here. The shop is open again. Father [Flip] is coming
home the 1st of May. He has recovered so much already. Isn't that wonderful? Toetie (the cat) is with
the neighbors, but Mary [a Jewish woman] cannot be
found anywhere. She must have missed her little
women so much that she ran away, but don't worry.
You will get another one. Be brave, and we'll meet you
again. We wish you lots of strength.

RONNY and COCKY

Dear Aunt Bep,

I am so happy that you can be at rest through all this, especially with the most difficult of all—Grandfather's passing away. We will be missing him very much and I have been very sad about it. But now I feel again the gratefulness for all he has been for us through all these years. His passing has been a motive for me to be baptized and make a profession of faith in the Reformed Church. I knew that he would have been very happy about this. The Bible text I used was: "What time I am afraid, I will trust in thee." It was very appropriate. Dear Aunt, be courageous. I am thinking often of you. Your nephew,

CASPER

Where Have the Children Gone?

A child was brought into the cell with her aunt. For half an hour her sad little voice sounded, "Daddy! I want to go to Daddy!" The next day that same little voice was singing, "The bells are ringing, the birds are singing." The lovely child's voice rose out above all misery and brought contact with the glory and praise of the Lord. Even that is possible!

Previously the same cell housed two even smaller children. Their voices sounded all day long, "Yes Mommy?" Normal children's sounds and expressions are so out of place here. It makes your heart shrink. But the little ones did not suffer from the cold cell. They stayed happy until in the night the guard came and took them away. Where to? After that it was even more quiet in that corridor.

. . . and so do I!

April 21st 1944

My Dear Kees [Corrie's nickname],

How happy we were with your letter and that the Lord has heard our prayers and you are at peace and happy. When I heard you were alone, I was so upset. Darling, now I have to tell you something very sad. Be strong. On the 10th of March, our dear father went to Heaven. He survived only 9 days. He passed away in Loosduinen. Yesterday I fetched his belongings from Scheveningen. I know the Lord will help you bear this. It was pneumonia. Bep knows it already, and wrote us about it. She had already had premonitions about this, years ago. She writes, "A person in whom Christ showed so completely to such full advantage, who lived so close to the Saviour, for whom the eternal things were so real, and who has all the conditions to become a martyr—and then I would think, 'He is not going to die in his bed.' God did not let His sovereignty slip from his fingers."

On Kierkegaard's tomb is written:

Only a little time and then everything is conquered.
Then the whole battle will all of a sudden be over.

Then he may drink from the water of life
And in all eternity speak with Jesus.

The Saviour will comfort you. We pray continually for you. Received a wonderful letter from Peter. Tine received notice that Willem will definitely come home [from prison] this week. The shop and repair shop are open. We are putting in a request [with prison authorities] for a family business appointment [with me and Bep].

Much has been stolen from the house and shop. Henri is in charge of the business. Flip will probably come home May 1st to go to school. Things are not so well with Mary. The others are fine. Come straight to us when you are free. How we will take care of you! Ask for permission to send us a request card for receiving parcel post. Otherwise parcels will not get through to you. May God bless you, my darling.

YOUR NOLLIE

P.S. Pray for me, too. It is more difficult for me now than when I was in Scheveningen.

Dear Aunt Kees,

How wonderful to hear from you! We got three letters at the same time, your letter, one from Peter, and Aunt Bep. Everybody is in good spirits. The watch shop is open again. A neighbor is taking care of Toetie but Mary seems to have run away. We cannot find her anywhere. That's a pity, but maybe Toetie will have kittens soon again. We wish you lots of strength. With lots of love from both of us.

RONNY and COCKY

Dear Aunt Kees,

How wonderful that you are so courageous, or better that God gives you so much strength, that you *can* be courageous. I have been baptized and have made a profession of faith. It was wonderful. The reason I did it was that I knew this had always been one of Grandfather's dearest wishes. Of course, it was sad that he could not be with us. The text [from the Bible] was, "What time I am afraid, I will trust in thee." It was a beautiful service. I am now a member of the Una Sancta to which my family in and outside prison, on earth and in heaven, also belong. That communion remains.

YOUR NEPHEW, CASPER

The Gift of Imagination.

A bird is softly singing a spring song. I can see the golden evening clouds through the 28 little panes of my window. And now my fantasy takes a flight: I see the sea, the white-capped waves. I really hear the murmur of the sea. The wind is from the West.

Betsie's at peace . . . .

E. ten Boom, cell 314

May 8, 1944

Dear Nollie,

Everything is well with me. Since I wrote on April 11 everything has improved. Physically as well as

spiritually I feel well. The atmosphere in the cell is
fine. My soul is very peaceful. Fortunately, I have
overcome the shock of the last months. I have trained
myself to concentrate my thoughts almost totally on
my cell and cell mates and to intensely share in their
ups and downs. In the beginning, I prayed for everything—everybody. I have learned not to do that anymore. I had to concentrate on Bible verses and medita-
tions, psalms and hymns which I remember. I only
knew parts of some but I still enjoyed them. I became
at peace in the long weeks of waiting till April 28 when
Mrs. Pigge [a friend from Haarlem] was put in our
cell. Last Tuesday I got into a conversation with her
about Haarlem and because of this my whole life
came clearly into mind again. Then Wednesday your
letter arrived. What a happiness and miracles. Casper's
profession of faith. The shop open again. Flip home.
My good glasses were on the counter.

Thursday, Friday, Saturday, and Monday I had to
go to a hearing. I signed the official report on Monday.
The interrogation is one miracle! Your prayers were
then, like always, around me. Every previous night
the Lord revealed to me what to say. It was not an
interrogation but a wonderful witnessing, telling the
motives for our acts. Because of this, I could constantly witness of the love and the redemption of the
Saviour, which I also always do in the cell.

I heard that Peter and Willem are free and that
Father was liberated on March the 10th. What a
liberation! The Lord leads me every minute and sec-

ond. That gives me courage now that I have to wait and wait. I am longing so much for you, for freedom, and for work.

I sleep as I have never slept in all my life. Aunt Jane says, "Aunt Bep is the favorite in sleeping." Corrie does not have to go to interrogations any more. I am so very grateful that I could take that for her but the dear child herself does not know this.

The friendship in the cell is such that one by one I have invited my cell mates to come to our house. Nollie, do you remember that in the corridor of the prison I said to you, "It looks like Möttlingen here"? Well, I have learned here at least as much as we did at Möttlingen. [Möttlingen is a little village in Germany where plain farmers taught the Bible. The counseling ability was known all over Germany and Holland.]

Fortunately I am still getting porridge and have had liver injections. Long live the Red Cross!

Don't forget: "Pray and give thanks."

YOUR BETSIE

"I am not afraid."

May 8, 1944

Dear Nollie and all other loved ones,

On May 3rd I received your letter. First I was sad, but now I am comforted completely. Father can now sing:

I cannot do without You,
You Jesus, my Lord,
Thank, praise, adoration,
Never will I be without You any more.

How beautiful his voice will sound. I am so happy for him. When I think of those 9 days I quickly switch to the present and concentrate on how happy he is now for he sees the answer to everything. On the wall of my cell is written in English, "Not lost, but gone before." He will leave a great emptiness in my life. For the love and help I gave him, the Lord will surely provide many others. But what I received *from* him can never be replaced. What a privilege though that we could for so long so *intensely* enjoy him. For a few days I was upset. Now that has passed. During the last few days there was such a tension within me. I did not dare to think things through and when you are so alone it is difficult to get away from your thoughts. Now that is gone and I am thinking much about the future. I make plans and am experiencing much peace. How good the Saviour is to me! He not only bears my burdens, He carries me, too!

I have signed my official reports but must still appear before the judge. I must also ask him for permission to either interrupt or terminate my punishment so that I can be treated in a sanatorium. I hope to come home this month or in any case in God's good time. Write and tell me how Lenie is, the girl who helped Elske with her homework. Give Hennie and Marie my regards.

How is Dirk from North Haarlem? [A man who helped to provide us with illegal ration cards.]

What a pleasure all the notes are. Every day I reread the letter at least once. I so hope you will succeed in obtaining the business interview. There is so much to be discussed. How wonderful, Casper, that you made a profession of faith. I know that you did it with all your heart. May God bless this step. Don't be concerned anymore about my being alone, Nollie. The Saviour is everything to me. Everything I lack He supplies.

My caseworker will see if I can have somebody to take care of me. That would be nice. Good that Willem is home again. Please write me as to how he and his children are doing. How wonderful the letter was that Bep wrote about Father. During our last few nights in our home, Father rang the bell to call me in the middle of the night for no reason except to talk for a moment. It was like a farewell and that is what I sensed it to be.

How is Mendlik's portrait of Father? Not damaged? Nice that Henri is managing the shop. Give him my regards, and Ineke and Hennie, too. Hennie, I know that you will give of the best you have to give and I thank you for this.

Wednesday I will receive a parcel postcard. Yes, Nollie, how difficult your path is, but the Saviour will give you a strong heart to go on at this time. I pray much for you. Please pray much for me. Bye, dear children and friends. God bless you all.

Would you please ask in the repair shop how the clocks of Eringa, Siertsema, Vermeer, Bulthuis, Smit, and Minnema are? [Names of underground people.]

When you bring a parcel to the Binnenhof, doesn't it get through? Please don't worry about it. I feel rather well. The hearing was not upsetting at all, for the Lord gave me such peace of heart.

Pray for guidance for me when I have to appear before the judge. I am not afraid. The Saviour never leaves me alone and He will not here either. Much love,

CORRIE

My Saviour Calms Me.

There is now no longer such a strong expectation in looking toward England—only when I look at the Saviour, does it become peaceful. Often I can give thanks that I may experience this but mostly there is a strong wish that it may be over. Now I really know what it means to cast my anxieties on the Lord when I think of Father. Is there still a future for the Beje here on earth or are we now going straight towards the return of Christ? Or are we going to die? How wonderful to know that the future is secure, to know that Heaven is awaiting us. Sometimes I have self-pity, especially at night, then my arm hurts very badly. This has to do with the pleurisy, but then I think of how much Jesus suffered for me and then I feel ashamed.

They worry about me . . . .

May 21, 1944

Dear Aunt Bep,
We all pray for you and for Aunt Corrie.

ELSKE

Dear Bep,
Received your letter of May 8. We are so grateful that you are so well, but long very much for your homecoming. Corrie writes, "I hope to come home this month." She writes again very cheerfully although she was very sad about Father's passing away. She writes that Father can now sing,

> I cannot be without You,
> You, Jesus my Lord,
> Thank, praise and adoration,
> Never will I be without You again.

"I am so happy for him," she writes. "If I think of those 9 days, I quickly switch to the present and concentrate on how happy he is now."

She was upset for a few days but now it has passed. She still had to appear before the judge to ask permission to be treated in a sanatorium. She did not write it openly, but we deducted that she has tuberculosis. Elly [doctor friend from Haarlem] said that the last time after she had pleurisy this also happened, but it got better soon and that usually, at her age, this is not something serious.

The shop was closed again after a few days and now Hennie and Ineke are in the shop of the optometrist next door. The portrait by Mendlik is on the mantelpiece in our front room. First I could not look at it—now I love to do so, but will be happy when it is hanging in the Beje again. Father's clothes and other belongings he had with him are also here. Never would I have thought that we would have to bear Father's passing away without helping each other, but now you have had only the Lord to turn to and you have experienced His help and support richly.

For what reason did you get those shots?

How wonderful that you sleep so well! And on such a hard mattress. Did you receive our parcel? You are getting another one with your glasses. I am hoping that these will be the right ones.

We can only ask for the business interview when we know who your new caseworker is. We will probably hear that this week.

                                        YOUR NOLLIE

Dear Aunt Bep,

How wonderful that you are so well. Aunt Kees also writes so cheerfully and is very interested in the shop. Asked about all the clocks of Bulthuis, Minnema,

Smit, and so forth, and I was happy that I could write her that they remained undamaged.

LOVE FROM ATY

Everything fine. All the others, except Henk are free. Best regards.

PIET

We pray for God's strength and blessing for you in these so difficult days. From Father, Mother, and Andy, also best regards.

MARIAN [a friend]

We are so happy that the letters which we receive are so cheerful and because we may trust that this cheerfulness is an answer to your and our prayers.

LENIE

Unsaved.

I am no longer alone but am with someone who is sentenced to death. A Jewish woman was pushed into my cell yesterday. I have told her in detail about the redeeming death of the Saviour. She does not accept it. Although she does pray, it is without life. She has no awareness of sin and spends her time reminiscing about all the wealth she had accrued and reproaching herself for not having managed things differently. She is bitter and dwells upon every unkindness of the guards.

6:00 P.M. We just had our inspection by the new *oberwachtmeisterin*, the head guard. Had to stand at at-attention ... I had too much food in my cell. In the adjacent cell, the prisoners remained seated. The *oberwachtmeisterin* snarled, "You are prisoners," and a moment later, "Do you think we are here for the fun of it?" A prisoner answered, "We sure aren't here for the fun of it either!" Prisoner was immediately taken to the "dark" cell. The other guards were shaken and inspected everything more thoroughly in order to curry favor. My plate and all the little tin cans and pots from my parcel were taken away. I don't know what to do with the apple butter (that was dumped out on my table). I was blessed that although the parcel was inspected in my presence, it was not taken away until later, for a little letter was in it.

Hate is such a bitter emotion, but I know that the Saviour with His cleansing blood is near me. The evil spirits cannot win.

At 9 P.M. my cell mate, Helen, was taken away. There was a heavy spiritual battle. She sat slumped over the table with her head in her hands. There was no ray of light anywhere in her. She seemed completely dark.

This morning I felt sick with misery but now I am quiet. Oh, how I enjoy the Psalms. I must once again adapt to being alone, but then, it is better than being with such a person I could not help.

"The clocks are undamaged . . . ."

May 21, 1944

Dear Aunt Corrie,

How are you? We all pray much for you and Aunt Bep.

ELSKE

Dear Kees,

Received your letter on May 17. We are so grateful that you both are well, but long for your return home. Mr. Kuhne was here. I am a little worried about your health. Write me, please. Tell me the exact details about it. Are you taking your temperature? It the doctor visiting you? Are you in bed?

Yes, Father's passing away will leave a great emptiness. He has been for us everything a father here on earth could be. We don't have a single bad memory of him.

His clothes are with us, as is the painting by Mendlik, which I love although I will be happy when it is hanging again in the Beje. Never had I thought that we would have to bear his passing away without being able to support each other, but your only resource was the Lord and you experienced His help and support richly. I had the same difficulty as you did at first. I was forced to continually think of those 9 days but then I concentrated on the glory which he is presently enjoying. Now it is no longer difficult for me and I can peacefully look at his portrait. Did the doctor tell you that you have TB? Bep is feeling very well. She has completely overcome the shocks of the last couple months. She was interrogated 4 days in a row. Each prior night the Lord gave her what she was to say and it became not a hearing, but a conversation to the glory of Christ as she testified to her love of the Saviour. She sleeps at night like she never slept before in her whole life. She is still getting porridge and received 3 shots—for what, I don't know.

She also writes that she is wonderfully at peace.

The parcel postcard has not yet arrived but this week another parcel is being mailed to you. Wasn't it nice last week?

The business interview can only take place when we know who your caseworker is. That we shall hear this week, I hope.

Willem and family are fine. The shop is closed again after a few days of being open.

Ineke and Hennie are working in the shop of the optometrist next door. Those people are very nice to us. God grant that you come home soon.

YOUR NOLLIE

Be of good courage, Jesus lives.
COR and ELLY

Your bed is already spread in a sanatorium. You can come right away. Everything is fine with Hendrik and Marie and also with Dick. All the people who were taken prisoner have already been freed. I asked Hennie about all those clocks about which you wrote. They are all undamaged.

A kiss from ATY

Everything well. Am very busy finishing the repair work that was still pending. Keep courage, Aunt.

PIET

Dear Aunt, be of good courage. Peter is very busy in the work for the retarded. All the best.

COCKY

P.S. Stien is in Arnhem.

Airing in Scheveningen.

I entered the garden gate. Don't think that it was like Florence Barclay's garden gate! This gate was a bolted door and when I had gone through it, I was once *again alone*. After 9 weeks, this was my first time outside. Red flowering shrubs, colorful little primroses, grass, yellow dunes, and a wide blue sky. My legs were stinging from their unfamiliar movement, but I walked and walked, on and on, on the rectangular path around the center lawn, and I drank in the colors and the air. Tremendous emotion made my heart beat faster, and then an unspeakable melancholy descended within me. I saw the colors through my tears. In me and around me was more loneliness than in the cell, and all of a sudden I did not see any beauty in the bare yard, but an atmosphere of death and cruelty. At the end, they had dug a long, narrow pit. It looked like a freshly dug grave. Half the shrubs were without leaves and were dead, like shrubs in Holland when they are planted in sandy soil. Around the yard was a high, hard wall with pieces of broken glass in sharp points lavishly cemented in its top, and in the north the tall prison, bare and cold with rows of barred windows. Near the south wall was the gruesome stench of burned bones and I could hear Christiaan telling me, "There are already three crematories in Scheveningen." Behind the south wall the rattle of a machine gun broke the silence. Then everything was, again, terrifyingly quiet. It was 2 o'clock and it was as if everything around me were a ghost city and I the only one alive. I walked on and an uncontrollable homesickness surged up in my heart. Even in the garden there was only loneliness for the solitary ones [those of us sentenced to solitary confinement].

Suddenly I remembered Enoch. He was not filled with homesickness when he walked with God and so I was no longer alone either. God was with me. Hand in hand, we walked on and saw the blue sky and the flowers and the flowering shrubs and I could see the yard as a part of a beautiful free world where I would be allowed to walk once again. In the same way, earth is a lonely garden and Heaven the Liberty where great joy awaits us children of the Light.

2

Vught

*"We don't know what
the future will bring,
but we are together."*

Transportation to Vught.

In the men's corridor I could hear them call, "All men, put on your own clothes." A moment later we hear in our department, "Be ready to take everything along." We don't understand anything that is happening. Hurriedly we gather all our belongings together, but it turns out that we have to wait for hours. At last we find ourselves in the corridor, two by two. A long row, the *Einzelhaften* [solitary prisoners], and the others, all alike. By bus to a small station. There we stand hour after hour. Behind us and in front of us, soldiers with their guns aimed and ready. *Wachterinen* [female guards], are running up and down in front of us. What is in store for us? Are we going to Germany? There are rumors about an invasion.

A train arrives and this causes confusion, which I use to edge over to the side. There I see Bep! When at last we are being loaded into the train, I hang back toward the side till I am next to Bep. We arrive together in a small compartment and sit next to each other. Night is falling and the train slowly moves on. Everywhere we have to wait. We are not allowed to have the windows open. Even so, two women and later, close to Den Bosch, a few men escape and they are searching with floodlights all around the train. We don't know where we are going or what the future will bring—but we are *together, together!* And we talk.

We have been separated for 3½ months and now the journey does not seem long, even though the trip actually lasts from 4 P.M. till 4 A.M. next morning. We tell each other everything. We talk and are together, *together!*

The train brings us very close to the concentration camp of Vught. There we climb down from the very high step of

39

the train. Ahead of us is a forest with many, many soldiers with helmets and machine guns all aimed at us prisoners, for there are hundreds of us, all occupants of Scheveningen, and the guards fear more escape efforts. Many floodlights are aimed at us and shine on the trees, the helmets, and guns—it seems like a gruesome movie. After waiting a long time, we are ordered to start walking in rows of five. We carry our belongings in pillowcases. One rips open and I hold my arm around it. We are being hurried on through the darkness. Swearing, raging, and yelling is all we hear. One soldier kicks several women in their backs because they try to avoid a big puddle. Oh, night of terror—but we are *together*.

Somehow this fearful march ends and we arrive in a large hall with straight benches without support, and there they leave us from 4 A.M. in the night till 4 P.M. the next afternoon—without supervision and—without food! But this last does not matter, for now there is a feeling of freedom and then, too, we are *together*. The moments are progressively worse. We have to shower and undress along with about 20 under one shower and, after this, we have to put on a prison dress and wooden shoes. Soldiers are walking around and the women have to wait a long time, naked. Bep and I put our arms around each other and we implore, "O Lord, not that, not that!" Then they call, "Stop bathing. There is not enough clothing." We shed tears of gratitude. Bep and I had not yet had our turn. Ten days later, when we are being supplied with these dresses, we are alone with friendly girls in the dressing room and then there is nothing menacing or ugly anymore. God answers prayers.

I am no longer *Einzelhaft*, but am together with 150 other women, but there is also multiplied suffering and fear in our barracks. A dear young Jewess approaches us and says, "Can you comfort me? I am so terribly scared."

The next ten days in Barrack #4 are difficult, but we are able to share and pass on the light of the Saviour. [We were next shifted into the official camp.]

Betsie's diary begins:

Tuesday, June 6

Unexpectedly brought to Vught in the night, to Barrack 4. Corrie and I were together in the train compartment. We immensely enjoyed it. Everything terribly strict here but still so grateful not to be in a cell any longer.

Thursday, June 15

Transferred into the camp here. We sleep, eat and sew side-by-side, and are now so happy! Both had physicals and are fine. Corrie's lungs fully recovered. Must get up at five each morning. Wear overalls and wooden shoes. Have fun walking on wooden shoes. We enjoy Lenie and Mien [Hennie's sister]. Each day and by night we are experiencing thousands of miracles.

Tuesday, June 20

Saw doctor. Had blood test. Spoke with Corrie. Got up half an hour earlier for long roll call. Shoes so quickly worn. Had Phillips-mash [camp food for people who work in the Phillips factory] and porridge.

Meanwhile, we hear from "home" at last:

June 20, 1944

My Dear, Dear Kees,

How happy we were this morning when we received the card with your number. Oh, my dear child, how I am longing for you. Every day we are waiting for you to come home. As yet, we have heard nothing from Bep. Oh, child, how I long to hear something from you personally. While you were still in Scheveningen, I knew exactly where your cell was and even all the guards. Now we don't know anything and all contact has been suddenly interrupted because of your departure for Vught. The only thing we know, and it is our great consolation, is that the same Lord, who looked after you in Scheveningen, is also with you now and will make everything right.

After we were together in Scheveningen, the notary and a few others went to see the gentlemen who are now in charge of your case, and the result was that the house and the shop were released. We went there immedately and cleaned the whole house. The shop is open and everything is waiting for you both. We have been absolutely assured that the letter for your release was sent some time ago.

Friday morning, June 9, we heard that you had left for Vught and in the afternoon Mr. Rahms phoned again to say that the letter, which will set you free, has been sent. We understand that because of all the bustle of transporting the whole prison, your case has been delayed, but you can also understand that we are constantly in suspense to know if you are coming home. You wrote once, "I won't stay here one moment longer than God wants me to." I think that maybe, you may still be a blessing to others or, perhaps you still have to learn something yourself. But I really would like to know how your health is and if you are still being medically treated and if you get extra food. I hope to send you a parcel soon. And Bep. We have not heard anything from her, but today we received notice to hand in your ration cards in the Zijlstreet. All we could find were the potato cards. We found more of the belongings remaining in the house than we had anticipated. Lenie is sleeping there every night. Mr. Rahms phoned to tell us that he is unable to find out where your caseworker is located. He knew only that the letter in question had been mailed, so now it is just a matter of patience.

Now, my dear child, God bless you and bring you back to us very, very soon.

YOUR NOLLIE

Dear Aunt Kees,

We here at home are all happy that you send such good news and are so well. Keep courage, Aunt. The last part is the hardest. Many regards from Mother.

AUNT JANNY and DICK

Dear Aunt Kees,

Also a little note from your caretaker of the retarded. I can tell you that they are doing well. Tomorrow, Stien and I will give them their first Bible lessons in the institute at the Zijlweg. It is a difficult time, but on the other hand also a wonderful time in which we learn so much about experiencing the power and love of our Saviour! I must also send you greetings from our church which shares in your suffering and prays much for you. It is really fantastic how people share with you in all this. Do you still remember how you told me, long ago, that it would perhaps become necessary for everybody to become evangelists? Well, maybe your wish has already partially come true now, although in a different way from what you had thought. Aunt, I wish you much strength and hope to see you again very soon.

YOUR PETER

Dear Aunt Kees,

Nice that we heard something again. Everything is fine here. All of us "turned the house with the broomsticks." It was quite a mess, but now everything looks spic and span again. Kindest regards and hope to see you soon.

YOUR COCKY

Dear Aunt Kees,

It is a fortunate coincidence that I can also write you, for I am home from Slootdorp just for a day.

Although I am far removed from the busy city life and even though it is unbelievably peaceful there, I often think of you and pray constantly for your speedy return home. We are all with you in our thoughts. I very much like living in the *polder*. The work is wonderful. I am working under a very pleasant pastor and learn much. I am also eating so well that I have gained 4 pounds already. However, it is very difficult for Kathy and me to be so far away from each other—especially for Kathy. She is still very weak and listless, and her nerves, which already were not very strong, have to endure a lot. The doctor diagnosed a general nerve weakness. Still, we will also come through this. Aunt, keep well. We keep trusting in our Saviour.

YOUR FRED

Dear Aunt Kees,

Nice that I may write a little note. I am staying at Aunt Nollie's for I have returned to Haarlem to stay. Tomorrow I am going evangelizing with Peter, which I like to do very much. The Damstreet inhabitants [my club girls] send their best regards. Annie is also fine. Well, Auntie, be strong. The Lord give you strength. Lots of love.

YOUR STIEN

Dear Aunt Kees,

Isn't it nice that the house has been released? We have already cleaned it for Aunt Bep, so that you will come home to a clean house. We have not yet heard from Aunt Bep, so we cannot write her. How do you like it there? We hope it's better than Scheveningen. Our family is doing a little bit of everything. It's so nice that Stien is here with us. Lenie is staying in a nice boardinghouse but she sleeps in her own bed in the Beje and can, at the same time, be the caretaker. Bye now, dear Aunt. Kindest regards from Piet. He is fine, works hard and is a bit tired.

A kiss from ATY

Betsie's Diary:

Saturday, June 24
Braiding terrible today. (Braiding of heavy rope is painful to the hands.) A nice walk with Corrie in the evening. Doctor took another blood sample.

Sunday, June 25
We had to report to sewing room. Fortunately I am being removed from the "braiding house of bondage." The morning flew by. In the afternoon, 50 of us gathered together outside. Wonderful! Then slept and did laundry. In evening, a discussion circle. Nice. Had a wonderful Sunday. Beautiful weather.

Monday, June 26

Sewing room. Saw doctor. Red blood cells
and leukocytes good. Shots twice a week.
Doctor gave me a whole bottle of glucose.
Atmosphere in doctor's office very kind. Sister
Hardenbrock [a nurse-baroness who was
also a prisoner] was very kind. [She didn't
survive.]

Barley not adequate so I got bread, *nu-*
trogen, and melba.

Tuesday, June 27

Yesterday someone gave a thimble to me.
Today a Belgian lady gave me a piece of
cake. Sewed socks. Yesterday the news was
very good. Some have returned from 's
Hertogenbosch (a nearby concentration
camp) and there were embraces and greetings when the Phillips work crew passed by.
Two especially were so happy to be back
here. Last night Corrie led the evening devotions. Again have hardly eaten a thing—
sauerkraut without potatoes, just in water.
A kind lady gave me a slice of bread with a
lot of butter. Tonight I had a slice of bread
with *nutrogen* and melba.

Wednesday, June 28

Glasses fallen apart again.

Friday, June 30

Yesterday, many blessings. Had a good talk with Smid. Went to doctor and dentist. Jan gave me butter and cheese. Red Cross sandwich with bacon. Washed a blanket. Cabbage soup. Evening devotions. Got my glasses back from Kuipers. They are glued. The sewing is nice. Am sleeping one bed back from window now since it is so cold in front of the open windows. Now more towards rear of barracks. Corrie is doing well at Phillips. Together we enjoy the beauties of nature, the skies, very much. The weather is cold. Just right. Every day some sunshine. We receive amazing strength for this harsh life. I am often suffering very much from hunger. Corrie brings a warm meal of Phillips' mash for me and I eat it while we stand at roll call.

"Hoed 10 hours."

July 2, 1944

Dear Everybody

[The "Everybody" here and in following letters means Nollie and anyone else at home who wishes news of us. The letter was to be shared.]

Bep and I are well. We are now working together and even sleep next to each other. We have gone

LOVED
ONES

Above: Here are some of our "watches" (code name for Jewish guests) in the Beje with underground workers.

Far Left: My beloved father, who said, "I am too old for prison life, but if that should happen, then it would be, for me, an honor to give my life for God's ancient people, the Jews." He died after nine days in prison.

Far Right: Willem, my only brother, who wrote to Betsie, "What a blessing when you may witness about Him by word and deed in surroundings where sorrow and privation open hearts so easily."

Left: My oldest sister, Nollie, who sent wonderful letters and packages to us in prison. It was Nollie who saved our notes—every scrap of paper—and gave them to me after the war.

Below, Left: My nephew Kik, Willem's son, who worked with the underground.

Right: Our beautiful Betsie who died at Ravensbruck. She wrote to Nollie, "The Lord leads me every minute and second. That gives me courage now that I have to wait and wait. I am longing so much for you, for freedom, and for work."

through very much, but life, side-by-side, is now very bearable.

Each week you may send a parcel. Send pencil, toilet paper, vaseline, sugar, Bep's shoes.

Bep is not healthy. Weighs 96 pounds.

Monday, June 12—worked in the fields. Hoed 10 hours.

Tuesday, June 20—in the morning we went to the sewing room. In the afternoon to the rope factory with ten others for a braiding detail. I got very hungry.

Wednesday—June 21—Again worked on braiding detail. Got a sandwich with bologna.

YOUR CORRIE

The Lord's Day.

It's Sunday evening in the barracks. Races are being held. The road has been lined off with strips of silvery paper for the event. A little child of about 3½ years is crying sadly. Her mother is Christian Reformed and considers it worldly to watch this on Sunday. I explain to her that, by this approach, she is sowing seeds of aversion where love should be sown. Fortunately, she is convinced and the little child radiantly watches the girls who are pushing each other in a wheelbarrow along the road, racing each other in sack-hopping, and other funny games. There is laughter, screaming, and applause. Suddenly, the gate opens and the guard dashes in. She is ranting and raving and immediately everybody gets *blocksperre,* which means that nobody may leave the block for the rest of the day and she promises us, "letter, package, and *blocksperre* ban" for at least a whole month. All of a sudden the grounds are empty and dead. I enter the dining room and expect grouching and complaining but that's not the case.

Everybody is eating or talking and in a happy mood. The expressions of the faces seem to say, "We have already suffered so much, we can take this in stride, too. We don't lose our courage. We keep our heads high."

Betsie's Diary:

Monday, July 3

Yesterday a wonderful Sunday. Sang in the sewing room. Spent afternoon with our friends. Then, we both wrote a letter, slept, and washed a blanket. Again, a gathering with our friends, and in Barrack 23, a concert of French, German, and Dutch songs. Such quality! Almost too beautiful! I had to cry when "Ach Wie So Bald" was sung. In between, we spent the time walking outside enjoying the nice, cool weather. We noticed that we are not as easily fatigued now as when we were first permitted to take walks.

This morning to the doctor. Got a shot and had a urine test made as I am abnormally thirsty and thin. My glasses broke again.

Tuesday, July 4

Yesterday evening both a letter and a parcel from Nollie. How good! Corrie had to read the letter to me. Her voice wavered and she had to stop several times. The letter for our

release was sent quite some time ago now.
The house and business have been released
and the condition of the house isn't too bad
. . . just as I expected from the Lord! Aty,
Cocky, and Mien cleaned the house. Stien
is also with them again and Lenie is there,
too. Everything is wonderful! . . . sausage,
cakes, fudge, sugar, cheese, etc. . . . What
an abundance! We almost had to let the
seams out on our nighties! [Of course, we had
no nighties!]

5 P.M. Thursday, July 6
Last night another parcel from Nollie.
How rich we are now that we have some
things to share with others! Yesterday, the
entire sewing room had a physical exam for
going to 's Hertogenbosch. Now, this morning, I had to go to the braiding detail again.
It was not too bad today although my thumbs
are burned raw from it. This afternoon I went
to the doctor. Urine check good.

Yesterday we washed a blanket together
again. Those dear girls from Groningen are
now in 's Hertogenbosch. Such a pity! Yesterday the children stood in a row in the open
field. They are darlings, all these beautiful
little children.

The Little *Doras*.

In the field in front of the hospital are lying in nice little cradles, the little *Doras*, fine healthy babies. The mothers work in the hospital. One of these, a sickly woman, had always had miscarriages and she had expected everything to go completely wrong here. But the finest gynecologist in the country, Dr. Heins, also a prisoner, was in charge of the hospital and everything went so well that mother and child turned out to be the happiest prisoners that you could imagine.

In the morning, the camp commander's car stops near the hospital and he gets out and plays with the children. He takes the little ones from their cradles and then he is just an ordinary human being, and one is not often allowed to be just that under the Hitler regime. When we march back to our barracks in the evenings, we pass the hospital and there they are standing, the three of them, each with a suntanned baby in her arms in that little field. This is maybe the most beautiful and also the most difficult moment of the day for all the mothers among us.

"We are aware that many are praying for us."

July 12, 1944

Dear Everybody,

Bep and I are well. Life is heavy, but healthy. I got vitamin B injections for my elbow. How beautiful are the Brabant skies. Please don't find it terrible that we are here. We can accept it ourselves. We are in God's training school and learn much. It is ten times better than being in a prison cell. Bep is aging fast, but fights her way courageously. She is brave. Letters and packages are high points. We are so happy to be together, especially when we grieve over Father. My lungs are healed. Write us how the children are going on. Bep is writing Nollie. Exchange these letters. Confer with Nollie how to send us woollen sweaters, also shoelaces, pillowcase, and strong towel.

We long much for freedom, but are unusually strengthened. Bep has gained 8 pounds! At the roll call often a skylark comes and sings in the sky above our heads, so we try to lift up our hearts. There is much fellowship of the saints here. Life is very simple. Everything is arranged for us, we never have to make a decision. We have nothing else to do but follow and obey. We enjoy little joys intensely. Great sadness we bear with God. We are aware that many are praying for us.

YOUR LOVING CORRIE

Flip.

Ours is a model medical facility and, thus, the most beautiful hospital of any located in the concentration camps. Ultraviolet lamps, message, diathermy, X ray, etc. —all are available. Our masseur is named Flip. Flip has a funny, round head. He, like all the other male prisoners, has been shaved bald. When we pass the hospital, he is always hanging out the window with his silly, bronze-colored head, calling merry greetings. I just now asked him if he could give pedicures. "For you I have everything! I can give you a pedicure, a manicure, or I can give you a spanking! I'll give you anything, only just don't ask me for cigarettes!"

"You cannot imagine what letters mean . . . ."

July 16, 1944

My Dear, Dear Nollie,

Yesterday we received your parcel and second letter written July 6. The first letter arrived July 4 and the first parcel July 5. Oh, how delicious everything is! You cannot imagine what parcels and letters mean to us. Everything you sent is useful, as was all you sent to us in Scheveningen . . . every bit of everything! I won't go into detail.

Nollie, we are completely at ease here. The Sundays are wonderful, for then we gather together with our friends. Often we exclaim, "Our family should see us now!"

I am sitting outside on a bench as I write. The men are playing soccer. We can hear them yelling on the other side of the fence. If there is any food left in the house, Nollie, please use it. Do please send us some condensed milk if there is any left . . . and cake, tomatoes, and more hairpins. Can you still buy everything?

Thea is here and she is well. Things are really quite good here. Life is hard but we receive needed strength. Miracles are happening. I don't feel myself to be a prisoner here as I did when I was confined to a cell. They treat you more like human beings.

Why did Stien leave so late and return so early? What is the matter with her? I knew the day of your silver wedding anniversary was approaching but couldn't remember the date. I can understand that you don't feel like celebrating it now. How sweet that you cleaned the house for us. I didn't know what to do about it, so that is a load off my mind. Are little clocks still there? [Meaning the Jews left hidden in the secret room.]

Corrie and I work in a factory, but then women all over the world work in factories! We are always full of courage except when, from time to time, I have trouble with my stomach and intestinal tract, but that seldom happens and it passes quickly.

We welcome butter. If you send bread, please don't preslice it and do please send something to put on it, also bouillon cubes, jam in unbreakable containers, loose sugar, preferably no lumps. We no longer receive Red Cross parcels but are permitted a parcel every 14 days. From your parcel I could tell that you received my letter.

Good that Elske is being allowed to take her exam. No letter from Willem yet. You received, in our letter of July 6, the answer to your letter of July 2.

Nollie, please write every week—one week to Corrie, the next to me. Thea sends her best regards. She is fine. I am homesick for Father.

BETSIE

Dreaming of Home.

It's hot and the blankets are terribly itchy. I close my eyes and dream of a bed with sheets. I am walking in our house in the Beje. I stroke the railing post at the foot of the stairs. I walk through the Liberty room and throw some wood on the fire. Then I look at Father's portrait and my closed eyes fill with tears. I think again of the 9 days which Father had to spend in that cell, but quickly I switch over and lose myself in thoughts of the glory of Heaven, which he is now enjoying. I am saturated with joy. We will meet again in God's time.

"Lots of strength . . . ."

July 23, 1944

My Dear Kees,

Received your letter of July 2. How wonderful that you both are so well. You have received our parcels in the meantime, I hope? We have sent them every week and this week Tine sent it. But now we have heard again that no parcels may be sent and that a letter may contain only 15 lines.

Bep's weight was a shock to me. Wonderful that you both feel so healthy. The Lord performed miracles on you that you recovered without being treated. I am longing so much for news from you and to know if the contents of the parcels are right. Oh, how we will spoil you both when you are home again!

Hennie and Ineke are going on vacation for a week. Lenie, who up to now slept in the house, has gone home. Now Peter is sleeping there. *Everything is all right there. Here too.*

Fred is preaching today in Oosterwietwert in N.O. Groningen, where they want to call him after he has passed his final exam in September. Bob took an exam in German. It was very difficult. Aty celebrated her birthday Friday. That's the reason I am late in writing. Peter is fine, studies hard, works much with the retarded. Cocky is working hard and Els is going to high school.

You received a long letter from Mr. Vos [a soldier who before the war found the Lord Jesus through Aunt Jans] which I answered. He had heard everything over there.

The butter you receive is always from Piet. I even got a box of chocolates from the lady in the Carel's shop and a sausage from the butcher across from you in the Beje. If only the mail ban will be lifted now!

I am copying the letters which were scribbled too closely. [Those written by me and sent on toilet tissue.]

Bye, my dear child. We pray much for you. Lots of love from your,

NOLLIE

Dear Aunties,

How wonderful that you are together. On July 26 I am going out with the retarded girls. I'm also going to Möttlingen Conference with Peter and Cocky, too. The girls in the Bible circle are going to Friesland. In the Beje everything is fine. Regards from Hennie, Ineke, and all the others. Lots of strength.

YOUR STIEN

Dear Aunt K.

Very happy I am to hear that you are doing well. Still happier we will be when you are first safe and sound in our midst again. In my thoughts, I give you a strong handshake. Hope to see you soon and best regards.

YOUR JANNY

Slave market.

We are still newcomers. Little things upset us. We do not yet understand that this concentration camp, in spite of all the cruelty, is not nearly as bad as a prison.

We do enjoy the fresh air, being able to walk outside, and having many people around us.

We are ordered to appear before the personnel in charge of the Phillips factory prison squad. In Barrack #2 we are waiting in the hallway to learn what kind of work we will be selected to do. The younger women have already been called up. The rest are over 40 and some are even 50 or older. The Germans despise the elderly.

We are sitting at the side and waiting. A group of men enter and keep standing in the center. One of them is the *Oberkapo*, or boss. He has thick lips and the lower lip protrudes, giving his face a cruel expression. He has beaten many Jews to death. Before the war, he was a professional killer and was himself sentenced to sixteen years. He got a lot of experience in brutality as a prisoner in the German concentration camps and he is now in charge of the Phillips prisoners. The other ones are nice, friendly people, but that we don't know yet, and while they are talking among themselves, looking at us and evaluating what kind of work we will be able to do, I feel suddenly like a slave on the slave market. They point at me and I am commanded to come to the front. A light shiver goes down my spine and, still, I experience this as something totally unreal. A young prisoner leads the way to Barrack #35 and he is teasingly telling me that I will have to do the most difficult work they can think of. This man [Jo Kruizer, later a good friend of mine—not the least for taking care of my shoes] is in charge of the sanitation unit here. He was a leader in the A.J.C. [Socialist youth movement] before his arrest. [I don't know if he came out alive.]

This moment on the slave market I will remember for a long time.

"We pray that the shoes will get through . . . ."

July 24, 1944

Dear Hennie,

How wonderful it will be to work together in the shop again. Oh, my child, that you now have to solve everything alone. I am so grateful to you and Ineke that you are doing this. I do not know any details, but I know that both of you are doing everything you can. Write please a card, or write to Mien [Hennie's sister] something about your experiences in the shop. She is just as much interested. Mien is brave and very good to us. During lunchtime she and I are always together, we work in different barracks but both for Phillips. She is healthy but skinny and most of the time she is brave. It is a hard life also for her, but it is much better than in the cell. There, she often had sick people to take care of. Here she is helping the nurse in the First Aid in the evenings and helps with dispensing medicines. She does all this voluntarily.

She often knows a way to obtain something when others don't know how to go about it.

Has business fallen off much because of the robberies? Or was it not too bad? Did we lose many customers or can you keep it going? Is ten Hove helping well? Do you get enough supplies? Where do you put the watches during the night? Are there still some supplies upstairs or is everything gone? Nice that you had a vacation. Did you still visit your family, Ineke? Oh, how I hope to see you soon. God bless you!

Nollie, you omitted the number. Bep is 01130 and I am 01131. Write every week even if Willem writes. It may pass through and you don't know how we enjoy it. The worst may be that the letter would not get through, then we would have bad luck. But still, then it's only the postage and the trouble of writing, that's wasted. And, if we are lucky we get it and the letter will be spelled out from A to Z, 10 times over. I am sorry at all, Stien, that you returned to Haarlem again.

Bob, congratulations on your preliminary success, and Elske now to high school. Aty, where did you stay in Holten? Did you have a nice time? Oh, Cocky, how nice about that conference. Nollie, how wonderful that you also are going to a conference. I am more worried about you than about ourselves, but that's not right. The Lord will give you strength, but oh, darling, what will it be when I can put my arms around you again!

I think now also that it will be September, then it will be 6 months. Because of the parcel blockade, we did not receive the fruit and shoes. We pray that the shoes and the sweaters may still get through. God does work miracles.

Enclosed is a diary by Bep and an embroidered cloth made by me in prison. We cannot take it along if we would be called from here. Oh, yes, also the letters to us are treasures.

YOUR CORRIE

Mrs. Hendriks.

In the washroom of Barrack 42 lies a bag with sandwiches. Mrs. Hendriks prepared them this morning to give to her husband who works in the same barrack as she does. She is a delicate woman with an unusual, fine, intellectual face. She also carries a baby under her heart, her first one. Last night Mr. Hendriks was shot to death.

Betsie's Diary:

Saturday, July 28

Wednesday was an inspection of the braiding detail for going to 's Hertogenbosch. I got a scare! Thursday, another inspection and a group let out Friday. During the morning, about 35 were called out to go to the Phillips factory but not me. In the late afternoon they called for volunteers for the dressing room. I applied for that. This morning I had to stand and wait in the cold for a long time and was then sent to the barrack to wait. When I got "home" to the barrack, all the beds were stripped and Barrack 24B was empty. We had to move to Barrack 23B. Here we sleep with 160 women in one room. The noise and the activity don't bother me at all. The dining room is also very crowded. There are many acquaintances and friends here. On Wednesday, Corrie was caught talking to a laborer and a note was made on her record. Let's hope this will not cause trouble!

This evening Corrie had to report to the office. Got a warning, nothing else. Everybody had said she would be put in the "bunker" [the worst building for punishment]. We had prayed until our fears left us and now we have been rescued from those fears.

In 23B, we have two nice beds on top with a beautiful view. We are continually protected by the most extraordinary Providence so that we can hold out in spite of the hard life. Last Sunday, a good conversation with Lenie. We have received no letters or parcels yet this week. The news we get continues to be good.

Wednesday, August 3

Sunday everybody was frightened. Friday a letter from Nollie. Everything is going well. Peter is sleeping in the house. Fred will probably be called to a pastorate in Oosterwiet-

wert. On Monday and Tuesday the prisoners'
boxes were inspected and much was taken
from us. Last night, after 4 weeks, a parcel
arrived. Corrie brought Phillips-mash, too.
There was nice porridge and an abundance of
buttered sandwiches from the parcel. I am
writing from the waiting room of the hospital
now, waiting for a *lauferin* or guard [one
whose duty is to escort prisoners]. I have
seen lots of people . . . the optician Zijlstra, Jo
who works in the kitchen, etc.

Friday they asked for volunteers to do sewing in the storage room where possessions of
prisoners are kept. There is such a kind,
considerate atmosphere there. We are treated
like elderly women. We sit in a small room
and sew on beautiful pedal machines. Each
of us has a hundred shirts and undershirts for
mending and I greatly prefer this to cutting
paper. There is also a cozy kitchenette and we
have 2 breaks for coffee, tea, and sandwiches.
We climb in and out of a window to go to the
bathroom, for the door is kept locked.

I should like to stay in the property room.
Corrie and I always enjoy the wonderful air
and clouds. The weather is excellent . . .
fortunately, not too warm. Mostly cloud skies
and cool, especially cool at roll calls. We have
only 2 blankets. Still, we don't catch colds.

It is August now and it smells so wonderful here. In the evenings, we have only a little while to enjoy ourselves. First, we eat together. Then there is the closing of the day with devotions, and finally, we wash and get quickly into bed. In the evenings, when we go to bed, it is still light and in the mornings when we get up it is still pitch-dark outside. We have a terrible lack of sleep and are tired but not overly tired.

Saturday I wandered around, first standing outside, then back to the barracks, and to the sewing room. In the sewing room Sunday morning, too. Wonderful morning! On the whole, a real Sunday!

"... a time of bliss."

August 9, 1944

Dear Beppie,

Thanks very much for your letter which gives us at last the opportunity to write to you. One card, which we sent you previously, was returned to me undelivered. Nice that the communication has been reestablished and also, that the parcels are getting through again. This week, Nollie was going to send a parcel. Next week, we hope to take care of it. I know what that means. Also what the world outside and the fresh air means. The lack of these last things is, in my opinion, harder to take than the lack of sufficient food.

How wonderful that you bring your problems to Christ and how invaluably wonderful it is to be in contact with Him! What a blessing when you may witness about Him by word and deed in surroundings where sorrow and privation open hearts so easily. As far as that is concerned, I can be jealous of you both when I think of the deeper comradeship which a camp like Vught produces. It seems as if His grace is working more instantly there, and as if God wants to fulfill His work there at an accelerated pace. Of course, we think daily of you. Tine and I always walk together in the forest from 7 to 8 every morning. We enjoy nature and this is a wonderful opportunity to bring our daily happenings to the Lord. We experience the result of this all during the day.

Last night (it was the evening before Casper's birthday, which we celebrated today) many young people in our home gathered together in our salon, most of them from non-Christian backgrounds, and all kinds of questions were asked. One of them, a medical student, reflected his final impression after the closing prayer, in the following purified language: "The pastor was darn good tonight."

As far as your prolonged stay is concerned, probably God still wants to teach you something. He wants to give you a new basis for work, in which you can utilize all the old knowledge again, and in which the same Christ is manifest but now in a quieter and broader way. Christ molds and models our work after the work of His Kingdom, which He is going to carry out on earth, and which none of us can yet sufficiently grasp.

When I was in prison in Scheveningen I composed a youth hymn, which I wanted to be completely free of politics. The third verse went like this:

> Young people, we were born for a future,
> In which again, we can spread our wings.
> For Satan long ago the battle was lost
> When he went bankrupt at the Cross.

> Quietly our King's business continues to win
> He wants us to take part and today to begin!
> A terrible time? No, a time of bliss
> Since Christ for His young ones the Victor is!

Regards, dear Beppie. Love to Corrie.

WILLEM

Dear Betsie,

How happy we are with your letters. We will take care of the parcels. We are grateful that you both are so well. Today we celebrate C's birthday and the day ended with an evening prayer, for you both of course. We are very busy but are enjoying God's rich consolation. How wonderful it will be when we all can be together again. But . . . we know so very little.

I hope that you will soon gain a few kilos and your blood count will increase, for that is necessary. It is fortunate that Corrie's lungs are healthy. Good-bye for now. From day-to-day we are with you in our thoughts. Kindest greetings,

YOUR TINE

A Day's Work.

In the Phillips factory most of us sit bent forward with heads on our arms. Outside the air is vibrating over the hot earth. I wear nothing but my overalls and the legs of those are rolled high. The door is flung open. Jan is trying to catch Janneke. They are holding large mugs of water in their hands which they throw across the work benches onto each other. Our tools and parts are totally disregarded. It becomes a wild romp!

Janneke is a big, dark, Belgian girl with laughing eyes and Jan is our foreman and a communist. The floor is soaking wet. Amidst much cheering, Jan and Janneke are both carried into the washroom by several of the others. Janneke is thrown into the sink and the faucets are turned on.

"Thick air" [Danger!] someone shouts. Immediately everyone resumes working quietly and, seemingly, diligently. The smiles are hidden. Janneke hurries to the bathroom and the cleaning girl mops the floor. Muller, the German officer, enters. Everything is so in order that he can find no reason for shouting or giving warnings. Muller's eyes are more piercing than ever.

"Send sweaters or something."

August 13, 1944

Dear Everybody,

Parcel and letter ban, but keep on writing. It may be lifted August 15 or September 1. Try immediately to send a parcel then. If you do receive this letter, write, "I received a letter from Kees."

Do you know how long our sentence will be? When we signed our statements, we saw that we had only been accused of helping Jews. They give you half a year for that. Does that start from March 1 or June 18?

We are fine, in good health, and like our work. I am working at the Phillips factory and Bep does sewing. We experience so many longings! When you find out how long [our sentence is] please write "I saw a little child of . . . months," and start counting from March 1.

Does it look like the war will be over soon?

When it's cold we don't have enough clothing. Send sweaters or something. We are only allowed to wear it under our overalls and most importantly send new shoes. Mine are completely worn out.

Jap and Stien take turns writing each week to Bep and me. We are able to witness here and there, but not nearly as much as we had expected. There is so much bitterness and communism, cynicism, and deep sorrow. The worst for us is not that which we suffer ourselves, but the suffering which we see around us. We also are learning to put the worst in the hands of the

Saviour. We are very tranquil, in rather good spirits, but not cheerful. Our health is fine. I gained 10 kilos. My hair has turned gray. Life is hard. It's as if I've been drafted into the army but in the harsh German way. But don't worry too much about that. In many aspects it's not too bad. Nollie, write much. Your letters help so much. More letters can get through now. Thank all those nice people. Don't ever make the parcels too heavy. Is Hans having financial problems? Congratulate her for me. God bless them. Send a picture of Father as a postcard. On the whole, I can accept quite well being here, but I have too many thoughts of home. I think often of Father. Yes, Jap, how wonderful that he is in Heaven. Nollie, how difficult things must often be for you, but you will receive amazing grace for this time. I pray for that continually.

In the morning we walk outside and pray aloud together. Everybody thinks that we are just talking, but then, we *are* just talking—talking with the Saviour, and that is such a joy. Bye darlings.

Keep courage! Cocky and Nol, my special regards.

CORRIE

The Prostitutes.

Pretty but nondescript faces, loud voices, saucy mannerisms. One always knows when the prostitutes are around. They never seem afraid. When everyone is standing in utter silence, listening to the threats and raging of our superiors, they call out daring replies. They know they are safe if the guards are men. They are the last to report for roll call. Some of them are always near the barbed-wire fence which separates us from the men's section. They sometimes climb up on the windowsills and we are warned at roll call to report anyone we see there. "Not all of you can be whores!" the guard yells. Late in the evening the little bell that hangs on the barbed wire tinkles innocently. A girl is climbing over the fence. "Mother," a fat woman and the eldest in the block, who is here for an abortion and is now in charge of 140 women, goes with the girl.

"He that is without sin among you, let him first cast a stone at her."

In the sewing room Bep sees that a lady is sewing a large round red piece of material on to a white square and this in turn is sewn on the back of a blue overall. It is for Mrs. Boosmans, who tried to escape and was caught with 2 others. As long as she will be wearing her overall, she will wear the red round cloth, the token of honor. She climbed over a few roofs, ran far away, was then caught and brought back; had to stand for hours and was not allowed to go to bed at night. She looks very tired, but seems not to worry. How brave she is! She just heard that her husband, Dr. Boosmans, was wounded in the train by shell splinters. He will have to lose a few fingers, but for the rest he is well. I have to say I am proud of our Dutch women.

Bep's birthday

August 19, 1944

Dear Everybody,

You must be asking what we did to deserve the parcel ban. It's a collective punishment. In our barrack the beds were not made neatly enough and much was hidden under the mattresses. Besides, some of the prostitutes had been talking with the guards through the window across the barbed-wired fence. Punishments are taken collectively. This will last till September 5. If by then we still are not home, send on that date a few parcels and before that time every week a good-sized parcel to Mien. She is sleeping in another barrack and therefore does not have the punishment. Keep on writing to us, and now and then also to her. Sometimes letters will slip through. On September 5, especially send heavy sweaters. When the mornings are getting colder we are not dressed warm enough. We have to be at roll call before sunrise. Oh, how beautiful the skies are then, but sometimes we are shivering with cold, if the weather is like autumn, chilly and foggy. At the moment we have a heat wave here. How I long for cool sheets and for much more. Will the end of the war be near? The world outside is at the moment not so attractive either. But even if it would be 10 times worse, we still long to go home.

Jap, will you maybe from my previous letters type the parts which are important for everybody? Pencil writing fades so easily. We are fine. It's Bep's birthday and what a much better day it is than mine was. Then [April 15] I was lying alone and was on cold food, no warm food and for the rest—no airing, no books. Everybody snarled and I felt so sick and miserable. A doctor gave me a shot and I told him that it was my birthday and then he gave me a firm handshake. He himself was a prisoner. Never did I appreciate a handshake so much as this one! The next day a corridor-girl came in front of my door and gave me congratulations from Aukje. Then, from her, I heard for the first time where Bep was. That was my first contact with Bep.

We sleep together now, Bep and I, and last night we woke up from the terrible flying over Vught. It sounded like thousands of airplanes. In the afternoon, I sleep for nearly an hour in the sunshine. One can admire here the most beautiful skies, heavenly beauty. We have enough to eat, are healthy, do like our work, many friends and acquaintances, and are healthy. I am very tanned and even Bep's face has a tan. She looks much better than some time ago and looks 10 years younger. My hand, in which I suffer from neuritis, is nearly better. I gained much weight. Just got a wasp sting on my leg, but I got a walking permit to go to the first aid a few barracks away. There I received a piece of cottonwool with some eau de cologne, but the nicest was the walk. Without a walking permit you are never allowed to leave your barrack.

Don't worry about us, that we would not have enough. Every time the Lord cares for us in a miraculous way, so that if we don't have anything, somebody gives us something. For instance, I went to the hospital for vitamin B and the cleaning girl gave me half a cake.

Did you know that Lenie den Engelsen is a cleaning girl in Barrack 42? Her husband is in 43. She works, mops, and is taking it beautifully. She is a heroine. How is it with Pickwick and Hans, Cocky and Henk, Jan, Ineke, and all the others? I pray much for all of

them. Also for Bob Weener. There is "summary justice"
here. If anybody passes on news or a notice, he gets
the bullet. Do you know if our prison time ends
September 1 or December 9? Everybody here says that
6 months at Vught is too short. If they also include the
time at Scheveningen, then it would be September 1.

God knows the way. We are at peace with everything. Write for sender, on the parcel to Mien, the
name and address of Jap or Fie.

Now that I read my letter again, it looks a little too
optimistic. It is very difficult for us but God's grace is
endless. Bep is often hungry, and is at the moment not
gaining any weight. Therefore, please send parcels
soon with the sweaters and shoes.

YOUR CORRIE

At Twilight.

It is evening. About 30 of God's children are standing
or sitting between the barracks. Two very old little women
with wooden shoes on their feet are sitting against a tree.
Bep is reading Psalm 91, "He that dwelleth in the secret
place of the most High shall abide under the shadow of
the Almighty." The light of the setting sun is shining on
her. She looks so pretty and even healthy [though very
chronically ill from pernicious anemia]. She is standing
there, bent over her little Bible. It's such a quiet evening. In a laundry room, two beautiful voices are singing
a duet from Mendelssohn. *"Denn in Seiner Hand ist, was
die Erde bringt."* ["For it is in His Hand, what happens on
earth."] The barracks are so ugly and the barbed wire so
horribly visible everywhere, but wagtails and skylarks are
sitting in the birch trees and over all this is spread God's

beautiful firmament with its magnificent colors which proclaim His handiwork.

"How long still?"

August 22, 1944

Dear Nollie,

I have written some sketches. Keep them for me. Will you send these letters on quickly? We hear some hopeful rumors. Could liberty be near? Oh, if it should be near, I hope we will be here [Vught] till the end, but also if they call me Monday the 28 or Thursday, I'll be tremendously happy, too. Oh, we are longing so much. Do you know yet when our time will be done? We have much peace about it. We miss our parcels very much and are hoping that you can send Mien van Dantzig our parcel. I once wrote you, "Don't send bread." But that was not good advice. If you don't slice it, then it stays delicious. Also, rolls are good. The crust prevents spoilage. Send *Haagsche Hopjes* [special Dutch candies] and write little notes on the thin paper inside the wrappers, but only in the ones in the bottom of the bag, for the guards steal them right in our presence. If we still have not been liberated by September 5, then please see to it that we receive a parcel with the shoes and a sweater in a separate package.

Many among us have stomach trouble, Bep is also suffering a little from it. Mien van Dantzig has had fever with it. Last night everything became just too much for her. She is usually so courageous. But this eventually gets to all of us.

I have found a dear friend in Mimi Lans, the daughter of Professor Lans.

Sunday we had about 60 people for our sermon. It's like there is an awakening. God's Spirit is working. Oh, if there could be a revival here! There is so much unspeakable anguish in this place.

Give my regards to Ellie and Kees Hage. Are they safe? There must be so much danger where you are, too! It is so wonderful that we can pray for you all the time. Oh, and Flip, is he in school as usual? And all the boys? When I come home I won't be able to stop asking questions!

Where is Bep's ID card?

Give my regards to Annie, Stien, Jap, Fie and all the others. Oh, Elske, how wonderful it will be to see you again. But Nollie, I long most of all for you. I do so hope that we may still enjoy being with each other for a long time to come. A half year is a long time, isn't it? But I believe that I have learned a lot.

I am no longer so tired in body and soul. Forgetting what lies behind I press on toward the goal for the prize of the upward call of God in Christ Jesus. It's the Saviour who has a task for us. He will lead us. Therefore how wonderful our life will be whatever the future may bring.

Piet, Aty, Leendert, Cocky—everybody—I so hope that we will be able to do some positive work together again in the future. I am longing for rest and for action at the same time. And on Sundays we will be singing again in the Liberty room [at home]. Here in the evenings we sing all the well-known songs so nicely when we close the day, and so often I think of Father—also of the Sunday afternoons at home.

How long still?

Club girls, be brave and work and help wherever you can. Bea, did you still get a chance to take an exam this year? Oh, how much I long to be in our clubhouse. But I am here and here is where I have to be and it is *well*.

We have a lot of sun here, much more than at home. I am writing at my workbench and in a little while Bep will be waiting for me and she'll get half of my Phillips-mash.

They say there'll be bag inspection, so first of all, everything has to be hidden well. Annie van Bavel, a communist, is walking around the workroom with a Jehovah's Witness to the beat of the whining music from the radio. Then all of a sudden a concert by Handel sounds through the workroom. How did the record get hidden in between that clamoring music? It was nearly too much for me! I did like Dr. Brouwer did when she was here and pressed my ear against the loudspeaker post to hear better. You may tell her this when you see her. See you.

YOUR KEES

Sharing.

The latrine is the most important room in the barracks, a space with 10 toilets, 3 or more of which are usually out of order and are covered with a large piece of cardboard, such as is used to cover the windows at night so no light can shine out for planes to see. In the camp, the latrine is the place where we have our most interesting political discussions. In the latrine, you comb yourself with a fine comb, you give secret messages or rest for a moment. You hide there when "the air is thick." [This phrase was used to warn that a guard was near.] Of course, when the danger is one of the female guards, this is no solution, for she follows you into the latrine, too.

You meet acquaintances in the latrine. You pass on dangerous news to others and you also do gymnastics. The latrine has 4 large open windows. There is one faucet over a little hole in the floor and that hole is always closed. Sitting next to each other in the latrine are communists, criminals, Jehovah's Witnesses, Christian Reformed, liberals, prostitutes. The bravest heroines who have made the greatest sacrifices are sitting there side-by-side with the degenerates of society.

Just a short while ago, right at lunch time, there was an air battle directly overhead. We lay in the sand watching. First, hundreds of airplanes flew over us like silver birds. They shone like diamonds in the sun's reflection. Then, suddenly, a crackling noise and shell fragments were flying all around us . . . bullets, too! We could not identify the planes. I ran and stretched out on the ground up against the barracks for shelter. I was not afraid and only later realized the seriousness of the moment. Five of us were wounded and have been hospitalized. Yesterday, somebody who had just arrived here from Barrack 4 said that everywhere over there in 4 you find underwear with our name, ten Boom, on them. [We always embroidered our underwear and shared it with other prisoners.] I pray that our words of consolation may also be shared. God's Word will not return empty.

"I am longing for all of you."

Bibi Kijzer, Bachplein 4. Amsterdam Z.

August 25, 1944

Dear Nollie,

Will you send the enclosed letters to the above address? A little note has been found—not on me—but we will have to be more careful.

During the last few weeks we have not heard anything from you. However, I hope and pray that you received our notes. Also, Mien has not received a parcel. Mien is completely well again. Bep looks a bit pale. Oh, may the Lord grant that we may come home soon. That would be more wonderful than I can imagine.

This morning Number 1 was called. She had been here the longest of us all. Even the guard, who brought the list from headquarters and apparently had not yet seen the numbers, exclaimed with some distress, "*Ach liebe, Numero Eins.*" The prisoner came forward from the group where we were standing in rows of 5 awaiting work commands. She swayed while she was standing in front of the office. We called to her, "Sit down, quick!" She dropped down on the uncomfortable bench made of birch trees, her arm on the back, her head on her arm. She was still sitting there when we marched away, "*eins, zwei, drei, vier.*"

The sun colored the clouds in the east so brilliantly that they illuminate us.

Leendert, will you copy the poems which are enclosed and send them on to Amsterdam? How is Dientje ten Boom? Give her my regards and, also Henri.

Oh, Bob, I long so much for you. Are you still studying German? I am longing for all of you, but we will be able to hold out.

"Daybreak in the east." It's such a blessing that this is such a beautiful month of August. Health by the spoonful!

Jap, will you type the portions of my letters which are important? Pencil writing fades so easily. You can decipher my scribbles. Is Rie Luitingh getting married soon? Give them my best wishes. His brother is fine. Also regards to Bob W.

My Bible verse for today is. "That I may see the good . . . . Lord, lift thou up the light of thy countenance upon us."

We cannot make the people here see the good in all this, but we can pray—Lift up Thy Light—Psalms 4:6.

YOUR CORRIE

This was my last letter from Vught. Shortly after I wrote it, many male prisoners were shot and killed. All women prisoners were transported to Ravensbruck concentration camp in the heart of Germany.

Bep and I were shipped to Ravensbruck on a

train. As we passed out of Holland we managed to slip a scrap of paper through a crack in our boxcar. The paper said:

> Corrie and Betsie ten Boom.
> Being transported to Ravensbruck concentration camp.

I asked the finder to please send the note to Nollie in Haarlem.

During my confinement in Ravensbruck, where mail was nonexistent, I felt a great emptiness. This was compounded when Betsie became one of 97,000 women to die there. When Betsie died in camp in the winter of 1944, she left this world with a smile on her face, the smile of one who knows the Saviour. She was gone, but I knew she experienced the happiness of Eternity.

The horrors of Ravensbruck, especially Betsie's death, caused me to wake up to reality. When I did, I was able to see that when all the securities of the world are falling away, then you realize, like never before, what it means to have your security in Jesus.

It was not until December 28, 1944, when, through a miracle, I was set free, just one week before all women my age and older were put to death. I was free and knew then as I know now it was my chance to take to the world God's mes-

sage of the victory of Jesus Christ in the midst of the deepest evil of man.

After being released from prison, I felt the need to write one final letter . . . to the person who had originally revealed our family's work to the Germans.

Haarlem, June 19, 1945

Dear Sir,

Today I heard that most probably you are the one who betrayed me. I went through 10 months of concentration camp. My father died after 9 days of imprisonment. My sister died in prison, too.

The harm you planned was turned into good for me by God. I came nearer to Him. A severe punishment is awaiting you. I have prayed for you, that the Lord may accept you if you will repent. Think that the Lord Jesus on the Cross also took your sins upon Himself. If you accept this and want to be His child, you are saved for Eternity.

I have forgiven you everything. God will also forgive you everything, if you ask Him. He loves you and He Himself sent His Son to earth to reconcile your sins, which meant to suffer the punishment for you and me. You, on your part have to give an answer to this. If He says: "Come unto Me, give Me your heart," then your answer must be: "Yes, Lord, I come, make me Your child." If it is difficult for you to pray, then ask if God will give you His Spirit, who works the faith in your heart.

Never doubt the Lord Jesus' love. He is standing with His arms spread out to receive you.

I hope that the path which you will now take may work for your eternal salvation.

CORRIE TEN BOOM

Afterword

The letters and notes in this book do not, of course, tell the whole story of what happened. I met many wonderful people while in prison, but because of the circumstances I do not have records of them to pass on. One person, however, does stand out in my mind. He is Hans Rahms, mentioned only briefly in 2 letters.

Hans Rahms was an official in Scheveningen prison during Betsie's and my interrogations. He was instrumental in helping my brother Willem be freed from Scheveningen after only a short stay. Willem was originally arrested with us at the Beje for teaching a Bible study.

But it was while we were in prison that the Lord touched Mr. Rahms's heart so that Betsie and I were both able to tell him about Jesus and His love. Later, in camp at Vught, Betsie told me that she had been able to say, "Mr. Rahms, it is important to talk about Jesus but it is more important to talk with Him. Would you mind if I prayed with you?" Five times she was ordered to report to this man for interrogation and five times she prayed with him . . . she, the prisoner and he, her judge. Through this, Hans Rahms became a friend instead of an enemy and we were recipients of his help several times during our imprisonment.

One morning, just before a hearing, he showed some papers to me. When I saw them, I knew that many lives were in great danger, for the papers contained detailed information about my underground activities. I could see on them the names of friends, Jews, and underground workers. When he asked me to explain the papers, I could not. The silence that followed was one of the most agonizing moments of my life. Then, suddenly, that moment was transformed into joy, for the judge took all the papers, opened the stove door, and threw them into the fire! Before my eyes, I saw the flames destroying every name and, at that instant, I understood the verse, Colossians 2:14, "Blotting out the handwriting of ordinances that was against us, which was contrary to us, and took it out of the way, nailing it to his cross."

That is what Christ did for us, and for me. After the war, I had the privilege of meeting Hans Rahms several times and he once said, "Corrie, I shall never forget your sister's prayers."

There were many things for which I needed to thank Mr. Rahms, for it was he who helped free my friends and some of my family from prison. Because he did many good deeds for people, it was difficult for him to see that he needed a Saviour, but, during one of our later meetings, he saw that he was a sinner and that he needed Jesus. Together we had experienced many dark moments and, occasionally, a light one, but the moment he accepted the Lord Jesus was one of life's richest experiences for me, for on that day I glimpsed a little of God's side of the pattern of my life.

God has only plans, no problems, in the life of a child of God.

I have experienced God's love.

> Love knows no limit to its endurance, no end to its trust, no fading of its hope: it can outlast anything. It is, in fact, the one thing that still stands when all else has fallen.
>
> 1 Corinthians 13:7, 8 PHILLIPS

Turn the page for an exciting
Special Preview of another book.

A Special Preview of
opening pages from Corrie ten Boom's
inspiring bestseller

THE HIDING PLACE

by Corrie ten Boom
with John and Elizabeth Sherrill

2

Full Table

It was 1898 and I was six years old. Betsie stood me in front of the wardrobe mirror and gave me a lecture.

"Just look at your shoes! You've missed every other button. And those old torn stockings your very first day at school? See how nice Nollie looks!"

Nollie and I shared this bedroom at the top of the Beje. I looked at my eight-year-old sister: sure enough, her high-buttoned shoes were neatly fastened. Reluctantly I pulled off mine while Betsie rummaged in the wardrobe.

At thirteen, Betsie seemed almost an adult to me. Of course Betsie had always seemed older because she couldn't run and roughhouse the way other children did. Betsie had been born with pernicious anemia. And so while the rest of us played tag or bowl-the-hoop or had skate races down frozen canals in winter, Betsie sat and did dull grown-up things like embroidery. But Nollie played as hard as anyone and wasn't much older than I and it didn't seem fair that she should always do everything right.

"Betsie," she was saying earnestly, "I'm *not* going to wear that great ugly hat to school just because Tante

Jans paid for it. Last year it was that ugly gray one—
and this year's is even worse!"

"Betsie looked at her sympathetically. "Well, but
. . . you can't go to school without a hat. And you know
we can't afford another one."

"We don't have to!"

With an anxious glance at the door, Nollie dropped
to her knees, reached beneath the single bed which was
all our tiny room would hold, and drew out a little
round hat box. Inside nestled the smallest hat I had
ever seen. It was of fur, with a blue satin ribbon for
under the chin.

"Oh, the darling thing!" Betsie lifted it reverently
from the box and held it up to the patch of light that
struggled into the room over the surrounding rooftops.
"Where did you ever——"

Mrs. van Dyver gave it to me." The van Dyvers
owned the millinery shop two doors down. "She saw
me looking at it and later she brought it here, after
Tante Jans picked out . . . *that.*"

Nollie pointed to the top of the wardrobe. A deep-
rimmed brown bonnet with a cluster of lavender velvet
roses proclaimed in every line the personage who had
picked it out. Tante Jans, Mama's older sister, had
moved in with us when her husband died to spend, as
she put it, "what few days remain to me," though she
was still only in her early forties.

Her coming had greatly complicated life in the old
house—already crowded by the earlier arrivals of Mama's other two sisters, Tante Bep and Tante Anna—
since along with Tante Jans had come quantities of
furniture, all of it too large for the little rooms at the
Beje.

For her own use Tante Jans took the two second-
story rooms of the front house, directly over the watch
shop and workroom. In the first room she wrote the
flaming Christian tracts for which she was known all
over Holland, and in the second received the well-to-do
ladies who supported this work. Tante Jans believed

that our welfare in the hereafter depended on how much we could accomplish here on earth. For sleep she partitioned off a cubicle from her writing room just large enough to hold a bed. Death, she often said, was waiting to snatch her from her work, and so she kept her hours of repose as brief and businesslike as possible.

I could not remember life in the Beje before Tante Jan's arrival, nor whose these two rooms had been before. Above them was a narrow attic beneath the steep, sloping roof of the first house. For as long as I could recall, this space had been divided into four truly miniature rooms. The first one, looking out over the Barteljorisstraat—and the only one with a real window—was Tante Bep's. Behind it, strung like railroad compartments off a narrow aisle, were Tante Anna's, Betsie's, and our brother Willem's. Five steps up from these rooms, in the second house behind, was Nollie's and my small room, beneath ours Mama's and Father's room, and beneath theirs the dining room with the kitchen tucked like an afterthought to the side of it.

If Tante Jan's share in this crowded house was remarkably large, it never seemed so to any of us living there. The world just naturally made place for Tante Jans. All day long the horse-drawn trolley clopped and clanged past our house to stop at the Grote Markt, the central town square half a block away. At least that was where it stopped for other people. When Tante Jans wished to go somewhere she stationed herself on the sidewalk directly in front of the watchshop door and as the horses thundered close, held up a single gloved finger. It looked to me more possible to stop the sun in the sky than to halt the charge of that trolley before its appointed place. But it stopped for Tante Jans, brakes squealing, horses nearly falling over one another, and the driver tipped his tall hat as she swept aboard.

And this was the commanding eye past which Nollie had to get the little fur hat. Tante Jans had bought most of the clothing for us three girls since coming to live with us, but her gifts had a price. To Tante Jans, the clothes in fashion when she was young represented God's final say on human apparel; all change since then came from the style-book of the devil. Indeed, one of her best-known pamphlets exposed him as the inventor of the mutton sleeve and the bicycle skirt.

"I know!" I said now as the buttonhook in Betsie's swift fingers sped up my shoes, "you could fit the fur hat right inside the bonnet! Then when you get outside, take the bonnet off!"

"Corrie!" Nollie was genuinely shocked. "That wouldn't be honest!" And with a baleful glance at the big brown hat she picked up the little fur one and started after Betsie round the stairs down to breakfast.

I picked up my own hat—the despised gray one from last year—and trailed after them, one hand clinging to the center post. Let Tante Jans see the silly hat then. I didn't care. I never could understand all the fuss over clothes.

What I did understand, what was awful and alarming, was that this was the day I was to start school. To leave this old house above the watch shop, leave Mama and Father and the aunts in fact leave behind everything that was certain and well-loved. I gripped the post so tight that my palm squeaked as I circled around. The elementary school was only a block and a half away, it was true, and Nollie had gone there two years without difficulty. But Nollie was different from me; she was pretty and well-behaved and always had her handkerchief.

And then, as I rounded the final curve, the solution came to me, so clear and simple that I laughed out loud. I just wouldn't go to school! I'd stay here and help Tante Anna with the cooking and Mama would teach me to read and I'd never go into that strange ugly building at all. Relief and comfort flooded me and I took the last three steps in a bound.

"Shhh!" Betsie and Nollie were waiting for me outside the dining room door. "For heaven's sake, Corrie, don't do anything to get Tante Jans started wrong,"

Betsie said. "I'm sure," she added doubtfully, "that Father and Mama and Tante Anna will like Nollie's hat."

"Tante Bep won't," I said.

"She never likes anything," Nollie said, "so she doesn't count."

Tante Bep, with her perpetual, disapproving scowl, was the oldest of the aunts and the one we children liked least. For thirty years she had worked as a governess in wealthy families and she continually compared our behavior with that of the young ladies and gentlemen she was used to.

Betsie pointed to the Frisian clock on the stairwall, and with a finger on her lips silently opened the dining room door. It was 8:12: breakfast had already begun.

"Two minutes late!" cried Willem triumphantly.

"The Waller children were never late," said Tante Bep.

"But they're here!" said Father. "And the room is brighter!"

The three of us hardly heard: Tante Jans's chair was empty.

"Is Tante Jans staying in bed today?" asked Betsie hopefully as we hung our hats on their pegs.

"She's making herself a tonic in the kitchen," said Mama. She leaned forward to pour our coffee and lowered her voice. "We must all be specially considerate of dear Jans today. This is the day her husband's sister died some years ago—or was it his cousin?"

"I thought it was his aunt," said Tante Anna.

"It was a cousin and it was a mercy," said Tante Bep.

"At any rate," Mama hurried on, "you know how these anniversaries upset dear Jans, so we must all try to make it up to her.

Betsie cut three slices from the round loaf of bread while I looked around the table trying to decide which adult would be most enthusiastic about my decision to stay at home. Father, I knew, put an almost religious importance on education. He himself had had to stop school early to go to work in the watch shop, and though he had gone on to teach himself history, theology, and literature in five languages, he always regretted the missed schooling. He would want me to go —and whatever Father wanted, Mama wanted too.

Tante Anna then? She'd often told me she couldn't manage without me to run errands up and down the steep stairs. Since Mama was not strong, Tante Anna did most of the heavy housework for our family of nine. She was the youngest of the four sisters, with a spirit as generous as Mama's own. There was a myth in our family, firmly believed in by all, that Tante Anna received wages for this work—and indeed every Saturday Father faithfully paid her one guilder. But by Wednesday when the greengrocer came he often had to ask for it back, and she always had it, unspent and waiting. Yes, she would be my ally in this business.

"Tante Anna," I began, "I've been thinking about you working so hard all day when I'm in school and——"

A deep dramatic intake of breath made us all look up. Tante Jans was standing in the kitchen doorway, a tumbler of thick brown liquid in her hand. When she had filled her chest with air she closed her eyes, lifted the glass to her lips and drained it down. Then with a sigh she let out the breath, set the glass on the sideboard and sat down.

"And yet," she said, as though we had been discussing the subject, "what do doctors know? Dr. Blinker prescribed this tonic–but what can medicine really do? What good does anything do when one's Day arrives?"

I glanced round the table; no one was smiling. Tante Jans's preoccupation with death might have been funny, but it wasn't. Young as I was I knew that fear is never funny.

"And yet, Jans," Father remonstrated gently, "medicine has prolonged many a life."

"It didn't help Zusje! And she had the finest doctors in Rotterdam. It was this very day when she was taken—and she was no older than I am now, and got up and dressed for breakfast that day, just as I have."

She was launching into a minute-by-minute account of Zusje's final day when her eyes lit on the peg from which dangled Nollie's new hat.

"A fur muff? she demanded, each word bristling with suspicion. "At this time of year!"

"It isn't a muff, Tante Jans," said Nollie in a small voice.

"And is it possible to learn what it is?"

"It's a hat, Tante Jans," Betsie answered for her, "a surprise from Mrs. van Dyver. Wasn't it nice of——"

"Oh no. Nollie's hat has a brim, as a well-brought-up girl's should. I know. I bought—and paid—for it myself."

There were flames in Tante Jans's eyes, tears in Nollie's when Mama came to the rescue. "I'm not at *all* sure this cheese is fresh!" She sniffed at the big pot of yellow cheese in the center of the table and pushed it across to Father. "What do you thing, Casper?"

Father, who was incapable of practicing deceit or even recognizing it, took a long and earnest sniff. "I'm sure it's perfectly fine, my dear! Fresh as the day it came. Mr. Steerwiljk's cheese is always——" Catching Mama's look he stared from her to Jans in confusion. "Oh—er—ah, Jans—ah, what do you think?"

Tante Jans seized the pot and glared into it with righteous zeal. If there was one subject which engaged her energies even more completely than modern clothing it was spoiled food. At last, almost reluctantly it seemed to me, she approved the cheese, but the hat was forgotten. She had plunged into the sad story of an acquaintance "my very age" who had died after eating a questionable fish, when the shop people arrived and Father took down the heavy Bible from its shelf.

There were only two employees in the watch shop in 1898, the clock man and Father's young apprenticeerrand boy. When Mama had poured their coffee, Father put on his rimless spectacles and began to read:

> "Thy word is a lamp unto my feet, and a light
> unto my path. . . . Thou art my hiding place
> and my shield: I hope in the word . . . ."

What kind of hiding place, I wondered idly as I watched Father's brown beard rise and fall with the words. What was there to hide from?

It was a long, long psalm; beside me Nollie began to squirm. When at last Father closed the big volume, she, Willem, and Betsie were on their feet in an instant and snatching up their hats. Next minute they had raced down the last five stairs and out the alley door.

More slowly the two shopworkers got up and followed them down the stairs to the shop's rear entrance. Only then did the five adults notice me still seated at the table.

"Corrie!" cried Mama. "Have you forgotten you're a big girl now? Today you go to school too! Hurry, or you must cross the street alone!"

"I'm not going."

There was a short, startled silence, broken by everybody at once.

"When I was a girl—" Tante Jans began.

"Mrs. Waller's children——" from Tante Bep.

But Father's deep voice drowned them out. "Of course she's going alone! Nollie was excited today and forgot to wait, that's all. Corrie is going with me."

And with that he took my hat from its peg, wrapped my hand in his and led me from the room. My hand in Father's! That meant the windmill on the Spaarne, or swans on the canal. But this time he was taking me where I didn't want to go! There was a railing along the bottom five steps: I grabbed it with my free hand and held on. Skilled watchmaker's fingers closed over mine and gently unwound them. Howling and struggling I was led away from the world I knew into a bigger, stranger, harder one. . . .

Mondays, Father took the train to Amsterdam to get the time from the Naval Observatory. Now that I had started school it was only in the summer that I could go with him. I would race downstairs to the shop, scrubbed, buttoned, and pronounced passible by Betsie. Father would be giving last-minute instructions to the apprentice. "Mrs. Staal will be in this morning to pick up her watch. This clock goes to the Bakker's in Bloemendaal."

And then we would be off to the station, hand in hand, I lengthening my strides and he shortening his to keep in step. The train trip to Amsterdam took only half an hour, but it was a wonderful ride. First the close-wedged buildings of old Haarlem gave way to separate houses with little plots of land around them. The spaces between houses grew wider. And then we were in the country, the flat Dutch farmland stretching to the horizon, ruler-straight canals sweeping past the window. At last, Amsterdam, even bigger than Haarlem, with its bewilderment of strange streets and canals.

Father always arrived a couple of hours before the time signal in order to visit the wholesalers who supplied him with watches and parts. Many of these were Jews, and these were the visits we both liked best. After the briefest possible discussion of business, Father would draw a small Bible from his traveling case; the wholesaler, whose beard would be even longer and fuller than Father's, would snatch a book or a scroll out of a drawer, clap a prayer cap onto his head; and the two of them would be off, arguing, comparing, interrupting, contradicting—reveling in each other's company.

And then, just when I had decided that this time I had really been forgotten, the wholesaler would look up, catch sight of me as though for the first time, and strike his forehead with the heel of his hand.

"A guest! A guest in my gates and I have offered her no refreshment!" And springing up he would rummage under shelves and into cupboards and before long I would be holding on my lap a plate of the most delicious treats in the world—honey cakes and date cakes and a kind of confection of nuts, fruits, and sugar. Desserts were rare in the Beje, sticky delights like these unknown.

By five minutes before noon we were always back at the train station, standing at a point on the platform from which we had a good view of the tower of the Naval Observatory. On the top of the tower where it could be seen by all the ships in the harbor was a tall shaft with two movable arms. At the stroke of 12:00 noon each day the arms dropped. Father would stand at his vantage point on the platform almost on tiptoe with the joy of precision, holding his pocket watch and a pad and pencil. There! Four seconds fast. Within an hour the "astronomical clock" in the shop in Haarlem would be accurate to the second.

On the train trip home we no longer gazed out the window. Instead we talked—about different things as the years passed. Betsie's graduation from secondary school in spite of the months missed with illness. Whether Willem, when he graduated, would get the scholarship that would let him go on to the university. Betsie started work as Father's bookkeeper in the shop.

Oftentimes I would use the trip home to bring up things that were troubling me, since anything I asked at home was promptly answered by the aunts. Once —I must have been ten or eleven–I asked Father about a poem we had read at school the winter before. One line had described "a young man whose face was not shadowed by sexsin." I had been far too shy to ask the teacher what it meant, and Mama had blushed scarlet when I consulted her. In those days just after the turn of the century sex was never discussed, even at home.

So the line had stuck in my head. "Sex," I was pretty sure, meant whether you were a boy or a girl, and "sin" made Tante Jans very angry, but what the two together meant I could not imagine. And so, seated next to Father in the train compartment, I suddenly asked, "Father, what is sexsin?"

He turned to look at me, like he always did when

answering a question, but to my surprise he said nothing. At last he stood up, lifted his traveling case from the rack over our heads, and set it on the floor.

"Will you carry it off the train, Corrie?" he said.

I stood up and tugged at it. It was crammed with the watches and spare parts he had purchased that morning.

"It's too heavy," I said.

"Yes," he said. "And it would be a pretty poor father who would ask his little girl to carry such a load. It's the same way, Corrie, with knowledge. Some knowledge is too heavy for children. When you are older and stronger you can bear it. For now you must trust me to carry it for you."

And I was satisfied. More than satisfied—wonderfully at peace. There were answers to this and all my hard questions—for now I was content to leave them in my father's keeping.

Evenings at the Beje there was always company and music. Guests would bring their flutes or violins and, as each member of the family sang or played an instrument, we made quite an orchestra gathered around the upright piano in Tante Jans's front room.

The only evenings when we did not make our own music was when there was a concert in town. We could not afford tickets but there was a stage door at the side of the concert hall through which sounds came clearly. There in the alley outside this door we and scores of other Haarlem music lovers followed every note. Mama and Betsie were not strong enough to stand so many hours, but some of us from the Beje would be there, in rain and snow and frost, and while from inside we would hear coughs and stirrings, there was never a rustle in the listeners at the door.

Best of all was when there were concerts at the cathedral, because a relative was sexton there. Just inside his small private entrance a wooden bench ran along the wall. Here we sat, our backs chilled by the ancient stone, our ears and hearts warmed by the music.

The great golden organ was one that Mozart had played, and some of its notes seemed to come from heaven itself. Indeed, I was sure that heaven was like St. Bavo's, and probably about the same size. Hell, I knew, was a hot place, so heaven must be like this cold, dank, holy building, where smoke rose like incense from the footwarmers of the paying customers. In heaven, I fervently believed, everybody had footwarmers. Even in the summer the chill never left the marble grave slabs on the floor. But when the organist touched the keys we scarcely noticed—and when he played Bach, not at all.

I was following Mama and Nollie up a dark, straight flight of stairs where cobwebs clutched at our hair and mice scuttled away ahead of us. The building was less than a block from the Beje, and probably a century newer, but here was no Tante Anna to wax and scrub.

We were going to see one of the many poor families in the neighborhood whom Mama had adopted. It never occurred to any of us children that we ourselves were poor; "the poor" were people you took baskets to. Mama was always cooking up nourishing broths and porridges for forgotten old men and pale young mothers—on days, that is, when she herself was strong enough to stand at the stove.

The night before, a baby had died, and with a basket of her own fresh bread Mama was making the prescribed call on the family. She toiled painfully up the railless stairs, stopping often for breath. At the top a door opened into a single room that was obviously cooking, eating, and sleeping quarters all at once. There were already many visitors, most of them standing for lack of chairs. Mama went at once to the young mother, but I stood frozen on the threshold. Just to the right of the door, so still in the homemade crib, was the baby.

It was strange that a society which hid the facts of sex from children made no effort to shield them from death. I stood staring at the tiny unmoving form with my heart thudding strangely against by ribs. Nollie, always braver than I, stretched out her hand and touched the ivory-white cheek. I longed to do it too, but hung back, afraid. For a while curiosity and terror struggled in me. At last I put one finger on the small curled hand.

It was cold.

Cold as we walked back to the Beje, cold as I washed for supper, cold even in the snug gas-lit dining room. Between me and each familiar face around the table crept those small icy fingers. For all Tante Jans's talk about it, death had been only a word. Now I knew that it could really happen—if to the baby, then to Mama, to Father, to Betsie!

Still shivering with that cold, I followed Nollie up to our room and crept into bed beside her. At last we heard Father's footsteps winding up the stairs. It was the best moment in every day, when he came up to tuck us in. We never fell asleep until he had arranged the blankets in his special way and laid his hand for a moment on each head. Then we tried not to move even a toe.

But that night as he stepped through the door I burst into tears. "I need you!" I sobbed. "You can't die! You can't!"

Beside me on the bed Nollie sat up. "We went to see Mrs. Hoog," she explained. "Corrie didn't eat her supper or anything."

Father sat down on the edge of the narrow bed. "Corrie," he began gently, "when you and I go to Amsterdam—when do I give you your ticket?"

I sniffed a few times, considering this.

"Why, just before we get on the train."

"Exactly. And our wise Father in heaven knows when we're going to need things, too. Don't run out ahead of Him, Corrie. When the time comes that some of us will have to die, you will look into your heart and find the strength you need—just in time."

Heartwarming Books
of
Faith and Inspiration

☐	11710	**THE GOSPEL ACCORDING TO PEANUTS** Robert L. Short	$1.50
☐	2576	**HOW CAN I FIND YOU, GOD?** Marjorie Holmes	$1.75
☐	10947	**THE FINDING OF JASPER HOLT** Grace Livingston Hill	$1.50
☐	10176	**THE BIBLE AS HISTORY** Werner Keller	$2.50
☐	12218	**THE GREATEST MIRACLE IN THE WORLD** Og Mandino	$1.95
☐	2866	**THE WOMAN AT THE WELL** Dale Evans Rogers	$1.50
☐	12009	**THE GREATEST SALESMAN IN THE WORLD** Og Mandino	$1.95
☐	2936	**I'VE GOT TO TALK TO SOMEBODY, GOD** Marjorie Holmes	$1.75
☐	10291	**THE GIFT OF INNER HEALING** Ruth Carter Stapleton	$1.75
☐	10405	**BORN AGAIN** Charles Colson	$2.25
☐	11012	**FASCINATING WOMANHOOD** Helen Andelin	$1.95
☐	12066	**TWO FROM GALILEE** Marjorie Holmes	$1.95
☐	11180	**LIGHTHOUSE** Eugenia Price	$1.75
☐	11189	**NEW MOON RISING** Eugenia Price	$1.75
☐	11291	**THE LATE GREAT PLANET EARTH** Hal Lindsey	$1.95
☐	11140	**REFLECTIONS ON LIFE AFTER LIFE** Dr. Raymond Moody	$1.95

Buy them at your local bookstore or use this handy coupon for ordering:

Bantam Books, Inc., Dept. HF, 414 East Golf Road, Des Plaines, Ill. 60016

Please send me the books I have checked above. I am enclosing $_____
(please add 50¢ to cover postage and handling). Send check or money order
—no cash or C.O.D.'s please.

Mr/Mrs/Miss_____

Address_____

City_____State/Zip_____

HF—6/78

Please allow four weeks for delivery. This offer expires 12/78.

BOOKS BEHIND THE LINES:

The side of war you will never read about in history books

☐	2501	**THE HOUSE ON GARIBALDI STREET** Isser Harel	$1.95
☐	12492	**THE WAR AGAINST THE JEWS** Lucy S. Dawidowicz 1933-1945	$2.95
☐	2858	**THE UPSTAIRS ROOM** Johanna Reiss	$1.25
☐	11405	**THE HIDING PLACE** Corrie ten Boom	$1.95
☐	11407	**THE PAINTED BIRD** Jerzy Kosinski	$1.95
☐	10619	**FAREWELL TO MANZANAR** Jeanne Wakatsuki Houston and James D. Houston	$1.50
☐	12347	**SUMMER OF MY GERMAN SOLDIER** Bette Greene	$1.75
☐	12510	**THE LAST OF THE JUST** Andre Schwarz-Bart	$2.95
☐	10482	**90 MINUTES AT ENTEBBE** Dan Stevenson	$1.95
☐	12097	**HIROSHIMA** John Hersey	$1.95